MODERN CONCEPTS IN CHEMISTRY

EDITORS

Bryce Crawford, Jr., University of Minnesota
W. D. McElroy, Johns Hopkins University
Charles C. Price, University of Pennsylvania

H. ZEISS, Ph.D., Columbia University, is President and Director of Monsanto Research S.A., Zürich. He has taught chemistry at Yale University and the University of Cincinnati and, as a National Science Foundation Senior Fellow, was Guest Professor at the Universities of Heidelberg and Munich. He is presently Adjunct Professor of Chemistry at the University of Zürich. Dr. Zeiss is the author of some fifty papers published in the professional journals.

P. J. WHEATLEY, D.Phil., Oxford University, is Staff Scientist, Monsanto Research S.A., Zürich. Dr. Wheatley was a Lecturer at the University of Leeds from 1950 to 1957, during which time he spent a year as Visiting Professor at the University of Minnesota. He spent the first half of 1965 as a National Science Foundation Senior Foreign Scientist Fellow at the University of Arizona. His papers have appeared in such publications as the *Transactions of the Faraday Society, Acta Crystallographica*, the *Journal of the Chemical Society*, etc.

H. J. S. WINKLER, Ph.D., University of Maryland, is Staff Scientist, Monsanto Research S.A., Zürich. He has been a Postdoctoral Research Associate at the Massachusetts Institute of Technology, Research Fellow at the University of Heidelberg, and a Postdoctoral Research Assistant at Iowa State University. Dr. Winkler has co-authored papers for the *Journal of Organic Chemistry* and the *Journal of the American Chemical Society*.

BENZENOID-METAL COMPLEXES

Structural Determinations and Chemistry

H. ZEISS
P. J. WHEATLEY
H. J. S. WINKLER

MONSANTO RESEARCH S.A., ZURICH

THE RONALD PRESS COMPANY • NEW YORK

Library of Congress Catalog Card Number: 66–21862
PRINTED IN THE UNITED STATES OF AMERICA

Preface

This work was undertaken in the belief that benzenoid-metal, or metal-larene, chemistry has progressed to the level at which a rational presentation of its subject matter can be made. To achieve this, we have restricted ourselves to transition metal complexes containing at least one benzenoid, or arene, group pi-bonded to the metal. This condition did not impose a severe limitation. It has, in fact, permitted us to deal in a definitive manner with that area of organometallic chemistry which has caused a certain amount of excitement during the past ten years.

Structural studies of the benzenoid-metal complexes have been brought together here for the first time. These contributions have proved to be indispensable to the progress of organometallic chemistry. The discussion of arene-metal carbonyl compounds is based on the extensive growth of new chemistry generated by research in this class of complexes during the past five years. Much of the dust of controversy surrounding the bis-arene-metal compounds has settled, and this has allowed a more dispassionate summary of this subject than would have been possible even a year ago. Literature coverage extends to January, 1965.

Finally, an attempt has been made to predict future lines of research that appear likely to bring special rewards in the years ahead.

We wish to acknowledge the patient assistance of Mrs. Vreni Jordi, who, in preparing the manuscript, has had to deal with three exasperating authors rather than one.

H. Zeiss
P. J. Wheatley
H. J. S. Winkler

Zürich, Switzerland
May, 1966

iii

Contents

Contents

BENZENOID-METAL COMPLEXES

I

Structure Determinations of Benzenoid-Transition Metal Complexes

INTRODUCTION

The number of benzenoid-transition metal complexes that have been investigated by means of single-crystal X-ray diffraction is relatively small. The complexes may be subdivided into three classes depending on the nature of the bonding between the arene and the other atoms in the crystal:

A. Complexes in which the arene is bonded by purely van der Waals forces, as in the benzene solvate of 1,2,3,4-tetramethylcyclobutadiene-nickel(II) chloride, $C_6H_6\{C_8H_{12}\}NiCl_2$ (15), or in the benzene-ammonia-nickel cyanide clathrate compound, $(C_6H_6NH_3Ni(CN)_2)_4$ (25).

B. Complexes in which a stronger force, such as charge transfer or polarization interaction, between the arene and the metal or other atoms operates, as in the benzene-silver perchlorate complex, $C_6H_6AgClO_4$, or the benzene-hexathiocyanatocobaltdimercury complex, $C_6H_6CoHg_2(SCN)_6$.

C. Complexes in which the arene definitely occupies one or more of the normal valency positions of the metal atom, and in which it may be assumed that a formal bond between the arene and the metal exists.

It should be noted that complexes in classes A and B are crystal compounds, and can exist as stable entities only in the solid state. In class C the possibility arises of true molecular compounds with a measure of stability in any state of aggregation.

As is frequently the case, these subdivisions are not rigid, and gradations between one class and another are bound to exist. However, with one exception, all benzenoid-transition metal complexes so far investigated fall unambiguously into one of these three classes.

We shall not be concerned with complexes in class A, since it is largely a matter of chance that an arene is present. Molecules other than arenes

3

would no doubt serve the same purpose of filling holes in the crystal structure, thus permitting stable crystals to be formed. Complexes in class B will receive a brief treatment, although it should be noticed that in no case is the metal involved strictly a transition metal. Complexes in class C will be discussed in detail. It is perhaps worth observing that there is only one example of a structure determination of a true σ-bonded benzenoid-transition metal complex (24a).

COMPLEXES INVOLVING POLARIZATION FORCES

The first recorded investigation of a benzenoid complex in class B is the benzene-silver perchlorate complex, $C_6H_6AgClO_4$, examined by Rundle and Goring in 1950 (26). The complete results did not appear until eight years later (28). Unfortunately, although the analysis was carried out with

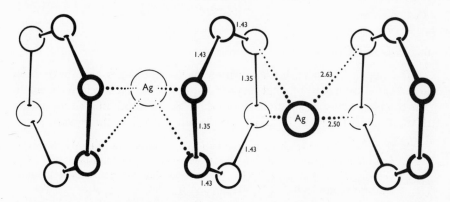

Fig. 1–1. The arrangement of silver ions and benzene molecules in the benzene-silver perchlorate complex.

as much care as possible, the reliability of the final results suffers from the presence in the crystal of disorder of the silver ions, and possibly of some of the oxygen atoms as well. The structure consists of perchlorate ions, and of chains of alternate benzene molecules and silver ions, with the perchlorate ions pushed away from one side of the silver ions to accommodate the benzene molecules. Two silver ions are associated with each benzene molecule, and *vice versa*. The silver ion positions are asymmetric with respect to the benzene rings. The Ag—C distances are 2.50 Å and 2.63 Å to the two carbon atoms of the nearest bond (see Fig. 1–1). The benzene rings appear to be distorted from the full $6/mmm$ symmetry, since the two C—C distances nearest the silver ions are 1.35 Å, whereas the other four are 1.43 Å. However, it should be remembered that the occurrence of disorder in the crystals, as well as the presence of the heavy silver ions, reduces the accuracy of the analysis, and it would be unwise to conclude from this structure determination alone that degradation of the symmetry of the benzene ring has been proved. The X-ray analysis has been criticized on the grounds of the high value of the second moment of the nuclear magnetic resonance spectrum at 77°K compared with that at 298°K (17,18). It has been concluded that the benzene molecules rotate "more-or-less freely" about the six-fold axis at room temperature. Such a criticism is misleading. The benzene molecules undoubtedly move; there is very probably some sort of rotation; but there is certainly not *free* rotation, since this implies that all orientations of the benzene molecules about the six-fold axis are equally likely, which is not the case. Free rotation can readily be detected by X-rays, and it is not detected here (27). A similar state of affairs exists, incidentally, in bis-benzenechromium(0) (24).

A structure that bears some similarities to the benzene-silver perchlorate complex is that of the adduct of benzene with hexathiocyanatocobaltdi-mercury, $C_6H_6CoHg_2(SCN)_6$ (19). The crystal consists of layers of the composition $(CoHg_2(SCN)_6)_n$ separated by benzene molecules. Each benzene molecule is associated with two mercury atoms, but each mercury atom with only one benzene molecule. The structure was solved and refined in three projections, and the accuracy is not high. The distances from each mercury atom to the two nearest carbon atoms of the benzene ring are 3.52 Å and 3.66 Å (see Fig. 1–2). The bond between the two carbon atoms nearest the mercury atom is, contrary to the situation in the benzene-silver perchlorate complex, found to be the longest bond, with a length of 1.49 Å. The lengths of the other two independent C—C bonds (the benzene molecule lies on a center of symmetry) are 1.40 Å and 1.37 Å. There is little doubt, however, that no significance can be attached to these differences in the lengths of the bonds in the benzene ring, and it must again be concluded that there is no proof of degradation of the symmetry of the benzene ring, though there can be no doubt that the interactions that enable the benzene molecules to hold the chains of $(CoHg_2(SCN)_6)$ together are rather stronger than van der Waals forces.

A third structure that may come into this class is the complex of benzene and aluminum tribromide, $C_6H_6Al_2Br_6$ (16). This can only be classed as a poor analysis, and the discrepancies between the lengths of Al—Br bonds that are expected to be chemically equivalent are such as to cast doubt on the correctness of the structure. The evidence for polarization bonding is slight, and, if it does exist, it occurs between the benzene molecule and bromine atoms.

A complex intermediate between classes B and C is the benzene-copper(I) aluminochloride complex, $\{C_6H_6\}Cu^IAlCl_4$. It is unique in that the metal is only four-coordinate (30). The cuprous ion is bonded to chlorine atoms of three different $AlCl_4^-$ tetrahedra at distances ranging from 2.36 Å to 2.56 Å. The distances expected for the sum of the normal covalent radii is 2.34 Å.

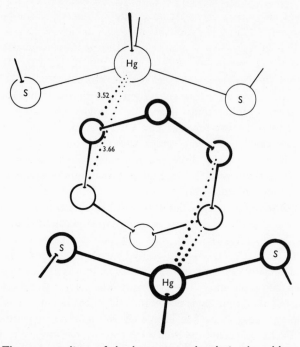

Fig. 1–2. The surroundings of the benzene molecule in the adduct of benzene with hexathiocyanatocobaltdimercury.

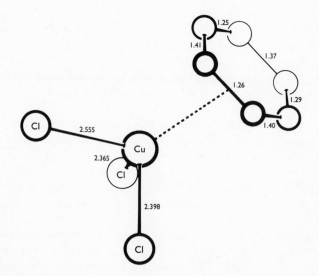

Fig. 1–3. The coordination of the cuprous ion in benzene-copper(I) alumino-chloride.

The angles between the Cu—Cl bonds are all considerably less than the tetrahedral value, one being $93 \pm 1°$, and the other two $102 \pm 1°$. Unlike the complexes in classes A and B, the metal ion is bonded to only one ring, and *vice versa*. The cuprous ion is not situated on the six-fold axis of the benzene molecule, and is not equidistant from the two nearest carbon atoms of the ring, the Cu—C distances being 2.15 Å and 2.30 Å (see Fig. 1–3). The analysis is a careful three-dimensional study carried out under favorable circumstances, and there appear to be strong indications that degradation of the symmetry of the benzene ring occurs. The distortion is toward a hexatriene system, long and short bonds alternating with lengths of 1.27 Å and 1.39 Å. It is one of the short bonds that lies nearest to the cuprous ion.

COMPLEXES INVOLVING VALENCY FORCES

Two related structures in class C illustrate the type of normal π-bonding that can be obtained with transition metals. Benzene-tricarbonyl-chromium(0), $\{C_6H_6\}Cr(CO)_3$ (1,6), and biphenyl-bis-[tricarbonyl-chromium(0)], $Cr(CO)_3\{C_{12}H_{10}\}Cr(CO)_3$ (2,7), have been investigated by X-ray diffraction, but unfortunately only in two dimensions. We understand from Professor L. F. Dahl of the University of Wisconsin that he has collected three-dimensional intensities from a crystal of benzene-tricarbonyl-chromium(0), and that accurate analyses of this and similar substituted complexes can be expected before long. There are many arithmetical errors in these papers, and all molecular parameters have been recalculated from the recorded cell dimensions and atomic coordinates, corrected when necessary for the omission of a minus sign. In both cases the reliability index R, the measure of agreement between observed and calculated structure factors for each reflection, is rather high, 18.5% and 17.0%. In the benzene complex, which is required by the space group $P2_1/m$ to have a plane of symmetry, the chromium atom is situated on the six-fold axis of the benzene molecule at a mean distance of 2.23 Å from each of the six carbon atoms. The C—C bond lengths are all very nearly equal with a mean length of 1.41 Å. The linear carbonyl groups form angles of 87° with each other, and are arranged *trans* with respect to the carbon atoms of the ring (see Fig. 1–4). The plane of the benzene ring is parallel to the plane containing the three oxygen atoms.

In the biphenyl complex, which is required by the space group $P\bar{1}$ to be centrosymmetric, the situation is rather similar. The six independent Cr—C distances probably do not differ significantly, and range in length from 2.20 Å to 2.34 Å with a mean value of 2.27 Å. There are indications that each phenyl ring is distorted toward a hexadiene system, but the differences in bond lengths are almost certainly not significant. The mean C—C distance within the rings is 1.41 Å. The rings are joined by a bond of length 1.48 Å. The carbonyl groups are linear and form angles of 88° with

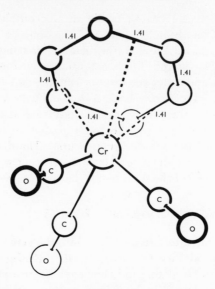

Fig. I–4. The structure of the benzene-tricarbonylchromium(0) molecule.

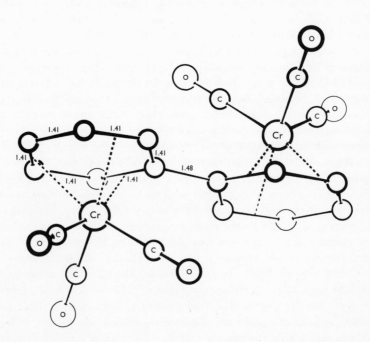

Fig. I–5. The structure of the biphenyl-bis-[tricarbonyl-chromium(0)] molecule.

each other.   They are nearly, but not quite, *trans* with respect to the carbon atoms of the phenyl rings (see Fig. 1–5).   The plane of the biphenyl molecule is parallel to the two planes, each of which contains the three oxygen atoms of a tricarbonyl group.

Yet a similar structure is that of phenanthrene-tricarbonyl-chromium(0), ${C_{14}H_{10}}Cr(CO)_3$ (14).   This is again a two-dimensional analysis, but the authors fully realize the limitations in the accuracy of the derived bond lengths.   The object of the investigation was merely to discover whether

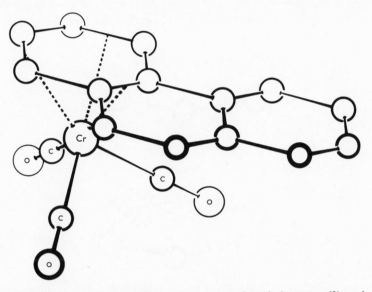

Fig. 1–6. The structure of the phenanthrene-tricarbonyl-chromium(0) molecule.

the chromium atom was bonded to an outer or the inner ring of the phenanthrene molecule.   It is found that an outer ring is preferred (see Fig. 1–6). There is no evidence of disorder, and such discrepancies as do exist in the lengths of the C—C bonds may all be ascribable to experimental uncertainty. The mean C—C distance in the ring π-bonded to the chromium atom is 1.43 Å.   The six Cr—C distances split into two groups, four centered around 2.17 Å, and two around 2.33 Å.   There is probably no significant difference between any of these values, and the mean of all six Cr—C distances is 2.22 Å.   The linear carbonyl groups form angles of $91 \pm 2°$ with each other, and are arranged *trans* with respect to the carbon atoms of the bonded arene ring.   The plane of the phenanthrene molecule is parallel to the plane through the three oxygen atoms.

Anthracene-tricarbonyl-chromium(0) has also been shown to have the chromium atom bonded to an outer ring, but further details are not available (13).

It is fair to say of all these analyses that, although they disclose no molecular disorder or deviation of the arene rings from $6/mmm$ symmetry, they are not sufficiently accurate to detect such relatively small effects if they are in fact present.

A molecule of the utmost interest is the parent bis-benzene-chromium(0), $\{C_6H_6\}_2Cr$. The main features of the molecular structure are not in doubt, as they are fixed by the minimum symmetry $\bar{3}$ which the molecule is required to possess in the crystal. Possession of this symmetry does not necessarily imply that the benzene rings are planar, since a crown form is consistent with $\bar{3}$ symmetry. However, it does demand that the mean planes through

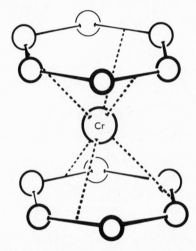

Fig. 1–7. The structure of the bis-benzene-chromium(0) molecule.

the six carbon atoms of each ring must be parallel, and must be normal to the line joining the centers of the rings through the chromium atom. Moreover, the benzene rings must be in the eclipsed position (see Fig. 1–7).

The real point of interest is whether or not the benzene rings have the full $6/mmm$ symmetry, and here the evidence is conflicting. The first investigation was undertaken by Weiss and Fischer (31), who, on the assumption of $6/mmm$ symmetry, derived a C—C distance of 1.38 Å and a Cr—C distance of 2.19 Å by trial and error. A more refined analysis by Jellinek (21), which gave very good agreement between observed and calculated intensities (R = 6.3%), showed that the molecule had the lower $\bar{3}m$ symmetry with alternating short and long bonds of length 1.353 Å and 1.439 Å. More recently Cotton, Dollase, and Wood (8), hereinafter abbreviated to CDW, who summarize the theoretical reasons for believing that no symmetry degradation should occur, concluded from a very careful independent study that there is no evidence for lowering of the symmetry, and that the C—C bonds are essentially equal at 1.387 Å. Jellinek (22) then refined his results still further with allowance for anisotropic thermal motion and maintains that alternating bonds are short and long with lengths of 1.366 Å and 1.436 Å. Finally Ibers (20) has treated CDW's data to intensive least-squares refinement, and has concurred with the original authors in believing that their data do not support degradation of the symmetry of the benzene molecule. Jellinek points out (22) that apparent $6/mmm$ symmetry could readily be achieved by a rather slight disordering of the molecules within the crystal, involving an apparent two-fold axis passing through the chromium atom and perpendicular to the rings. Such an orientational disorder is not unexpected with molecules of high symmetry placed in symmetrical surroundings.

The question now arises: Why, in the substance that has been most exhaustively examined, should this critical difference arise? It must be remembered that it is only because the structure has been so carefully studied that these relatively small differences in molecular structure can even be discussed. In most of the molecules dealt with previously the errors were such that no significance could be attached to differences of the present magnitude.

Before judgment is passed on the relative merits of the two analyses, one important point should be noticed. Because of the high symmetry of the cubic space group $Pa3$ to which crystals of bis-benzene-chromium(0) belong the chromium atom contributes only to those planes which have all three indices odd or all three even. The intensities of planes with mixed odd and even indices arise only from the contributions from the carbon and hydrogen atoms, and are therefore relatively weak. Jellinek measured the intensities of 177 independent reflections, of which only 29 had mixed indices. CDW, on the other hand, measured 267 reflections, of which 83 had mixed indices. On this basis alone, CDW's analysis should be the more reliable.

The difference between the two sets of results can be due to only two causes: either there is, as Jellinek suggests (22), a real difference between the two crystals that were exposed to the X-ray beam, or rather slight differences in the mechanics of the refinement, such as different observed structure factors, different scattering factors, different weighting schemes, or different numbers of reflections, have had an effect rather greater than would normally be expected. In an attempt to settle this question, we have carried out a thorough analysis of the two sets of structure factors, one published by Jellinek (22), and the other supplied by Professor Cotton. Of the 267 planes observed by CDW and the 177 by Jellinek (now abbreviated to J), 174 planes are common to the two sets. Table 1–1 shows a list of agreement factors R, defined as $R = \sum | |F_1| - |F_2| | / \sum |F_1|$, for the two sets of data before additional refinement was begun.

TABLE I–I

Comparison of J's and CDW's Observed and Calculated
Structure Factors Before Additional Refinement

F_1	F_2	No. of Planes	R
CDW (obs)	CDW (calc)	267	4.9%
J (obs)	J (calc)	177	5.3
CDW (obs)	J (obs)	174	7.2
CDW (obs)	CDW (calc)	174	4.4
J (obs)	J (calc)	174	5.3
CDW (obs)	J (calc)	174	5.0
CDW (calc)	J (obs)	174	7.0

The important features in this table are, first, that the agreement factor between the two sets of observed data is 7.2%; secondly, that J's calculated structure factors agree better with CDW's observed data than they do with his own; and finally, that the R factors are consistently lower with CDW's observed data than with J's. These three facts suggest that CDW's measured intensities are, throughout, more accurate than J's.

We have next carried out seven least-squares refinement cycles for each set of 174 common reflections under precisely similar conditions. The starting point was the arithmetic mean of CDW's and J's final atomic coordinates and isotropic temperature factors. The calculations were carried out on an Elliott 803 computer with a least-squares program that employs the block-diagonal approximation (12). A Cruickshank weighting scheme was used (9). The scattering factor for the chromium atom was corrected for dispersion, and anisotropic thermal factors used for all five atoms in the asymmetric unit. The final agreement factors were 5.3% for J's data and 3.3% for CDW's, again indicating that the latter are more reliable. The final thermal parameters, except for the hydrogen atoms, did not differ greatly, suggesting that thermal motion or disorder cannot be greatly different in the two crystals. The derived bond lengths with their standard deviations, both before and after this additional refinement, are summarized in Table 1–2.

TABLE I–2

Derived Bond Lengths Before and After Additional Refinement
(all lengths and standard deviations in Å)

	J	CDW	J	CDW
$C_1—C_2$	1.3656	1.3891	1.3582	1.3873
σ	0.0116	0.0073	0.0133	0.0069
$C_1—C_2'$	1.4358	1.3996	1.4418	1.4118
σ	0.0116	0.0073	0.0133	0.0069
Difference (Δ)	0.0702	0.0105	0.0836	0.0245
σ	0.0201	0.0126	0.0230	0.0120
Δ/σ	**3.49**	**0.83**	**3.63**	**2.04**

The important feature here is the last row. Before additional refinement the difference between the lengths of the two independent C—C bonds is highly significant with J's data, and not significant with CDW's. This, of course, is the basic discrepancy between the two sets of results. After comparable refinement with 174 common reflections, J's difference in lengths remains highly significant, whereas CDW's has now become possibly significant, all significances being evaluated on the Cruickshank and Robertson scale (10). The increase with CDW's data can only be due to a restriction in the number of planes. It seems to us, therefore, very likely that the apparent discrepancy between the two original analyses is not due to a difference between the two crystals examined, but results from a combination of the two circumstances emphasized above, namely that CDW had more planes and more accurate intensities. This conclusion cannot be considered certain, and there is little doubt that the whole question of the structure of bis-benzene-chromium(0) will soon be resolved by a low-temperature study currently being undertaken by Jellinek (23). Meanwhile the problem remains an intriguing one.

Another approach to the solution of the problem of symmetry degradation in π-bonded arene complexes has been tried by Bailey and Dahl (3), who have carried out a three-dimensional analysis of hexamethylbenzene-tricarbonyl-chromium(0). Full details are not yet available, but a preliminary announcement (4) indicates that there is no evidence of a three-fold distortion. However, there is a marked distortion towards a hexadiene system with two shorter bonds of length 1.37 Å and four longer ones of length 1.44 Å. The arene ring and its substituent carbon atoms are planar. This distortion is in marked contrast to that suggested by Jellinek (22) for the parent bis-benzene-chromium(0).

The only structure analysis of a benzenoid-chromium complex in which the metal is not in the zerovalent state is that of bis-toluene-chromium(I) iodide $[\{C_7H_8\}_2Cr^I]^+I^-$ (29). The molecule is required by the space group $I2/m$ to have $2/m$ symmetry, so that the analysis is a very straightforward one. The account is rather sparse in details, neither a list of structure factors nor an agreement factor being given. The analysis appears to be a reliable one, but the presence of the heavy iodine and chromium atoms must necessarily reduce the precision with which the carbon atoms can be located. Thus the quoted estimated errors of ± 0.01 Å for the Cr—C and ± 0.03 Å for the C—C distances are probably too low. The required molecular symmetry determines the general structure of the cation (see Fig. 1–8). The mean Cr—C distance is 2.08 Å. The C—C distances are very nearly equal, with a mean value of 1.42 Å. There is no evidence of symmetry degradation in the arene ring. The methyl group is attached to the ring by a bond of length 1.49 Å, and the only unexpected feature is that the methyl group is not coplanar with the rest of the ring. It is bent away from the

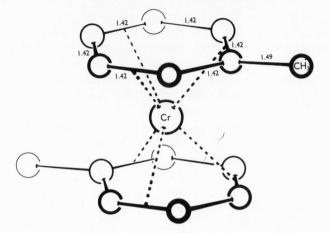

Fig. 1–8. The structure of the bis-toluene-chromium(I) cation.

remainder of the cation through 4°, presumably by repulsion from the nearest carbon atom of the other ring, which lies at a distance of only 3.5 Å.

The final molecule to be described in this section is hexakistrifluoro-methylbenzene-cyclopentadienyl-rhodium(I), $\{C_6(CF_3)_6\}\{C_5H_5\}Rh^I$ (5). The analysis is a very careful three-dimensional study. The cyclopentadienyl group is attached to the rhodium in the normal way by three π-bonds. The arene, on the other hand, appears to be attached by one π-bond and two σ-bonds (see Fig. 1–9). The σ-bonded carbon atoms are at a distance of 2.15 Å from the rhodium atom, whereas the carbon atoms involved in π-bonding are at a distance of 2.04 Å. The C—C bond involved in π-bonding has a length of 1.45 Å, whilst the non-coordinated double bond on the opposite side of the ring has a length of 1.32 Å. To complete the picture, the arene ring is folded across its center line so that the two halves make an angle of $48 \pm 2°$ with each other.

This example illustrates very forcibly the magnitude of the symmetry degradation that may be encountered, for one reason or another, in benzenoid-transition metal complexes.

We are left, therefore, in the position that the arene rings in some of these complexes appear to show no, or only very slight, departure from $6/mmm$ symmetry; others show a small but definite departure toward either a hexadiene or a hexatriene system; and in one the degradation is so enormous that one is left wondering whether there was ever an arene there in the first place. We can only agree with Professor Dahl (11) that it is necessary to accumulate accurate experimental information for a variety of molecules in order to be able to unravel the various contributing factors and assign degrees of importance to the many conflicting interactions which must determine the structures of these benzenoid-transition metal complexes.

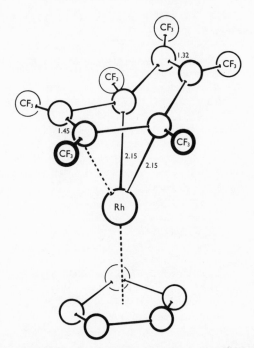

Fig. I–9. The structure of the hexakistrifluoromethylbenzene-cyclopenta-dienyl-rhodium(I) molecule, with the fluorine atoms omitted.

We thank Professors L. F. Dahl, F. A. Cotton, and F. Jellinek for preliminary disclosures and for discussions of their results, and Dr. J. J. Daly for helping to assess the reliability of the various X-ray structure determinations.

REFERENCES

1. ALLEGRA, G., *Atti Accad. Naz. Lincei, Rend. Classe Sci. Fis. Mat. Nat.*, **31**, 241 (1961).
2. ALLEGRA, G., *Atti Accad. Naz. Lincei, Rend. Classe Sci. Fis. Mat. Nat.*, **31**, 399 (1961).
3. BAILEY, M. F., and L. F. DAHL, *Abstracts*, 148th Meeting Am. Chem. Soc., No. O-66 (1964).
4. *Chem. Eng. News*, Sept. 21, 1964, 50.
5. CHURCHILL, M. R., and R. MASON, *Proc. Chem. Soc.*, **1963**, 365.
6. CORRADINI, P., and G. ALLEGRA, *J. Am. Chem. Soc.*, **81**, 2271 (1959).
7. CORRADINI, P., and G. ALLEGRA, *J. Am. Chem. Soc.*, **82**, 2075 (1960).
8. COTTON, F. A., W. A. DOLLASE, and J. S. WOOD, *J. Am. Chem. Soc.*, **85**, 1543 (1963).
9. CRUICKSHANK, D. W. J., D. E. PILLING, A. BUJOSA, F. M. LOVELL, and M. R. TRUTER, *Computing Methods and the Phase Problem in X-ray Crystal Analysis*, Pergamon Press, New York, 1961, p. 32.

10. CRUICKSHANK, D. W. J., and A. P. ROBERTSON, *Acta Cryst.*, **6**, 698 (1953).

11. DAHL, L. F., private communication.

12. DALY, J. J., F. S. STEPHENS, and P. J. WHEATLEY, unpublished results.

13. DEUTSCHL, H., Diss. Thesis, München (1962), quoted in B. R. WILLEFORD and E. O. FISCHER, *Naturwissenschaften*, **51**, 38 (1964).

14. DEUTSCHL, H., and W. HOPPE, *Acta Cryst.*, **17**, 800 (1964).

15. DUNITZ, J. D., H. MEZ, O. S. MILLS, and H. M. M. SHEARER, *Helv. Chim. Acta*, **45**, 647 (1962).

16. ELEY, D. D., J. H. TAYLOR, and S. C. WALLWORK, *J. Chem. Soc.*, **1961**, 3867.

17. GILSON, D. F. R., and C. A. McDOWELL, *J. Chem. Phys.*, **39**, 1825 (1963).

18. GILSON, D. F. R., and C. A. McDOWELL, *J. Chem. Phys.*, **40**, 2413 (1964).

19. GRØNBAEK, R., and J. D. DUNITZ, *Helv. Chim. Acta*, **47**, 1889 (1964).

20. IBERS, J. A., *J. Chem. Phys.*, **40**, 3129 (1964).

21. JELLINEK, F., *Nature*, **187**, 871 (1960).

22. JELLINEK, F., *J. Organometal. Chem.*, **1**, 43 (1963).

23. JELLINEK, F., private communication.

24. MULAY, L. N., E. G. ROCHOW, and E. O. FISCHER, *J. Inorg. Nucl. Chem.*, **4**, 231 (1957).

24a. OWSTON, P. G., and J. M. ROWE, *J. Chem. Soc.*, **1963**, 3411.

25. RAYNER, J. H., and H. M. POWELL, *J. Chem. Soc.*, **1952**, 319.

26. RUNDLE, R. E., and J. H. GORING, *J. Am. Chem. Soc.*, **72**, 5337 (1950).

27. SMITH, H. G., *J. Chem. Phys.*, **40**, 2412 (1964).

28. SMITH, H. G., and R. E. RUNDLE, *J. Am. Chem. Soc.*, **80**, 5075 (1958).

29. STAROVSKII, O. V., and Y. T. STRUCHKOV, *Dokl. Akad. Nauk SSSR*, **135**, 620 (1961).

30. TURNER, R. W., and E. L. AMMA, *J. Am. Chem. Soc.*, **85**, 4046 (1963).

31. WEISS, E., and E. O. FISCHER, *Z. Anorg. Allgem. Chem.*, **286**, 142 (1956).

2
The Arene π-Complexes

INTRODUCTION

The chemistry of the π-bis-arene metal complexes now rests on a sufficient number of experimental facts to allow an attempt at definitive description. Powerful physical methods have been applied to structural investigations of these complexes; the results have not been disappointing. The preparatory area of arene π-complexes has been broadened by new methods and a further development of the original ones. The mechanism of their formation, however, remains largely unknown, and continuing study of this phenomenon is providing an introduction to a body of chemistry intimately related to new concepts of catalysis.

Reactions of the arene π-complexes have been examined generally and are disappointing in the sense that they are limited. It may be hoped of course that this situation will be changed by original effort. Meanwhile, the bis-arene complexes must be viewed as "dead end" compounds.

METHODS OF PREPARATION

Grignard Synthesis (Fr. Hein)

The method employed by Hein (79) in the first preparation and isolation of organochromium compounds retains its importance. Although important modifications must now be incorporated, the procedure still consists essentially of reaction of a transition metal halide with aryl Grignard at temperatures below 0°, with complete exclusion of oxygen and moisture. The experimental modifications, however, are critical: solvent, stoichiometry, and temperature.

The synthesis of bis-arene-chromium complexes by the Grignard method has been separated into three distinct processes by careful attention to the experimental modifications just mentioned (93). Chromium(III) chloride or chromium(III) chloride tris-tetrahydrofuranate (94) reacts with phenyl Grignard in an *exact* ratio of 1:3 in *tetrahydrofuran* at −25°:

(1) $CrCl_3 + 3\ C_6H_5MgBr \rightarrow (C_6H_5)_3Cr \cdot 3\ THF + 3\ MgBrCl$

The σ-bonded triphenylchromium(III) may be isolated as the red crystalline compound just formulated or as a combinative salt with magnesium halide, *i.e.*, $(C_6H_5)_3Cr \cdot 3\ MgBrCl \cdot 6\ THF$ (95).

Triphenylchromium(III) tris-tetrahydrofuranate is next stripped of tetrahydrofuran by washing with diethyl ether, or by vacuum, or with warming. In all of these events the red substance is converted *irreversibly* into a black pyrophoric material whose composition is presently believed to be that of a mixture of π-complexed structures; for, on hydrolysis under nitrogen, hydrogen is evolved and the zerovalent bis-arene-chromium π-complexes are liberated:

(2) $3\ (C_6H_5)_3Cr \cdot 3\ THF \xrightarrow[\text{Et}_2\text{O}]{-3\ \text{THF}}$ Intermediate

(3) $\Big|\begin{smallmatrix}\text{N}_2, \\ \text{H}_2\text{O}\end{smallmatrix}$

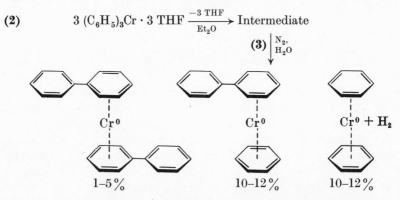

1–5%   10–12%   10–12%

Hydrolysis with exposure to air gives these same complexes in the monovalent state. It is clear from reaction **2** why previous attempts to prepare organochromium(III) compounds such as triphenylchromium from Grignard reaction in diethyl ether failed (7).

The mechanism of the transformation of σ-bonded arylchromium to bis-arene-chromium π-complexes is not understood. Clearly an oxidation-reduction process has occurred in the hydrolysis step (145). Quite recently, Hähle and Stolze (74) have contributed new information which bears on this problem. They find that a selective removal of tetrahydrofuran from triphenylchromium(III) tris-tetrahydrofuranate can be accomplished either by subjecting the crystals to a stream of argon or by treating them with *n*-heptane, benzene or diethyl ether:

$$(C_6H_5)_3Cr \cdot 3\ THF \rightleftharpoons (C_6H_5)_3Cr \cdot 2\ THF + THF$$
red   green

Further, complete removal of tetrahydrofuran either by further washing with benzene or diethyl ether gives the black intermediate (reaction **2**) from which bis-biphenyl-chromium(0) can be extracted *prior* to hydrolysis. However, bis-benzene-chromium(0) and biphenyl-benzene-chromium(0) can be obtained only *after* hydrolysis.

These results are in agreement with our earlier work in which deuterolysis of the black intermediate incorporated deuterium only into the benzene components of the "sandwich" complexes and not into the biphenyl layers (147). It is further to be noted that the preferential removal of one tetrahydrofuran molecule from the tris-tetrahydrofuranate concurs also with other indications that the coordinated tetrahydrofuran molecules in tri-phenylchromium(III) tris-tetrahydrofuranate are not equivalent and that the three phenyl groups differ in reactivity (*cf.* Cyclic Condensation). For these and steric reasons this σ-bonded organochromium compound is formulated in the *trans*-configuration. Chromium(III) tribromide tris-tetrahydrofuranate is known from crystallographic study to exist in the *trans*-form (22), although of course it does not follow that the triphenyl derivative must have the same geometry:

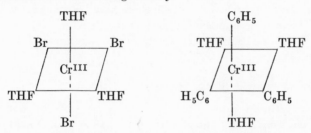

Also, the considerable amount of biphenyl appearing as a component of the π-complexes or in the free state when chromium(III) trichloride is reacted with phenyl Grignard in refluxing ether arises from the juxtaposition of two phenyl groups within the triphenylchromium(III) complex.

A favorable situation for ligand group interaction is presented by the tribenzylchromium(III) molecule. Whereas this σ-bonded organochromium derivative is stable in tetrahydrofuran, it rearranges in diethyl ether to produce the π-complex of 2-benzyltoluene and toluene in *ca.* 5% yield (71) and free 2-benzyltoluene as well. The point to be especially noted in the formation of 2-benzyltoluene is the *hydrogen transfer* process required in the coupling reaction:

$(C_6H_5CH_2)_3Cr(III) \xrightarrow{(C_2H_5)_2O} \xrightarrow{H_2O}$

H_2 + 2-Benzyltoluene + Toluene + Bibenzyl

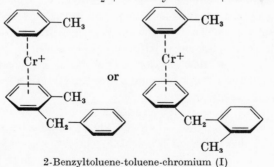

2-Benzyltoluene-toluene-chromium (I)

Deuterolytic studies of this reaction have demonstrated that the *ortho*-hydrogen atom of a benzyl group has been transferred internally over the chromium center and that part of the toluene has been formed by hydrogen transfer also (123a).   The section on Ruthenium contains a striking example of tautomeric transfer of hydrogen within a complex (16a).

The hydrogen transfer process has been observed also in the preparation of arene-π-complexes from acetylenes (*cf.* Cyclic Condensation) and is a phenomenon closely related to the catalytic properties of metal centers.

The Grignard synthesis of arene π-complexes has been used successfully with other transition metal halides.   However, the course of reaction is even less well known than with chromium halide on account of greater difficulties in handling the intermediates.   While there may be similarities in forming first the σ-bonded organometallic derivative, there must be considerable differences in the rearrangements which follow.   Certainly this is a fruitful area for investigation.

The Aluminum Method (E. O. Fischer, W. Hafner)

The Fischer-Hafner process for synthesizing bis-arene π-complexes from arene hydrocarbon, aluminum powder, metal halide, and aluminum chloride is superior to other methods when the aromatic reagent is either unsubstituted or substituted with groups unreactive under Friedel-Crafts conditions. The reaction was originally carried out in a bomb tube at 140° in preparing bis-benzene-chromium, thereby placing the bis-arene-chromium π-structure on the solid foundation of rational synthesis (39):

$$3 \ CrCl_3 + 2 \ Al + AlCl_3 + 6 \ C_6H_6 \rightarrow 3[\{C_6H_6\}_2Cr][AlCl_4]$$

The π-complexed cation was then reduced with dithionite ion:

$$2[\{C_6H_6\}_2Cr]^+ + S_2O_4^{-2} + 4 \ OH^- \rightarrow 2\{C_6H_6\}_2Cr^0 + 2 \ SO_3^{-2} + 2 \ H_2O$$

Fischer and Seeholzer (60) have devoted considerable attention to this reaction and have greatly improved the simplicity, yields, and applicability of the process.   The use of a large (seven- to eight-fold) excess of aluminum chloride has an optimum effect on yield of π-complex.   The bomb tube has been replaced by the reflux column, and the reduction step to zerovalent π-complex can be eliminated by direct alkaline hydrolysis of the reaction mixture.   Aluminum bromide, but not the fluoride or iodide, is also effective as catalyst in this reaction.   Triethylaluminum may be used in place of the aluminum halide/aluminum powder mixture, a result which has been overlooked in some quarters.

The path of the reduction of transition metal halides by aluminum in the presence of aluminum halides and aromatic hydrocarbons has not been clear. The paper by Fischer and Seeholzer deals extensively with this matter in the case of $Al/AlCl_3/CrCl_3/C_6H_6$.   The question which arises is to what extent is

Cr^{III} reduced by aluminum powder. Originally, Fischer and Hafner (40) formulated a reduction of Cr^{III} to Cr^I with π-complex formation according to the above equation, giving $[\{C_6H_6\}_2Cr][AlCl_4]$. We have contended that the reduction is complete, $Cr^{III} \rightarrow Cr^0$, since hydrolysis of the reaction mixture under nitrogen gives bis-benzene-chromium(0) directly, although in smaller yields (145). Further experiments have shown that bis-benzene-chromium(0) itself undergoes reaction with aluminum chloride in the presence of benzene (83,84), essentially the conditions of the Fischer-Hafner process, and that the product is the same as that isolated from the process itself before hydrolysis:

$$3\{C_6H_6\}_2Cr^0 + 8\ AlCl_3 \rightarrow 3[\{C_6H_6\}_2Cr^I][AlCl_4] \cdot 4\ AlCl_3 + Al^0$$

It is also shown that the bis-benzene-chromium(I) cation undergoes disproportionation during alkaline hydrolysis:

$$2\ [\{C_6H_6\}_2Cr^I]^+ \rightarrow \{C_6H_6\}_2Cr^0 + Cr^{+2} + 2\ C_6H_6$$

Herein lies the explanation of our experimental results and also support for the contention that Cr^{III} is indeed reduced initially to Cr^0.

The Fischer-Hafner process for preparing bis-arene π-complexes has been applied generally to transition metal salts with success. Some modifications of the method are required, depending upon the metal salt being reacted, and these are described under the particular metal headings in the following sections. The aromatic compound employed must be inert toward aluminum halide, as stated earlier. For example, an attempt to prepare bis-chloro-benzene-chromium from chlorobenzene resulted in halogen elimination and formation of the bis-benzene-chromium π-complex (15).

The influence of aluminum chloride or bromide on the formation of π-complexes, as noted before, is profound. Hein and Kartte (82) have found that the arene components of the bis-arene-chromium π-complexes may be thermally interchanged in the presence of aluminum halide. For example, biphenyl-benzene-chromium has been converted into bis-benzene-chromium and bis-biphenyl-chromium under these conditions. These conversions, for example, are reversible:

$$\{C_6H_5C_6H_5\}\{C_6H_6\}Cr + C_6H_5C_6H_5 \underset{}{\overset{AlCl_3}{\rightleftharpoons}} \{C_6H_5C_6H_5\}_2Cr + C_6H_6$$

the position of equilibrium being dependent as usual on the effective concentration of the reaction components.

Fischer and Seeholzer (60) have taken advantage of this phenomenon in ameliorating the conditions of the Fischer-Hafner process. Addition of a catalytic amount of mesitylene to the $Al/AlCl_3/CrCl_3/C_6H_6$ system, for example, reduces the required temperature markedly. This effect is attributed to the ease of formation of bis-mesitylene-chromium, which then undergoes rapid interchange of aromatic components with benzene:

$$\{(CH_3)_3C_6H_3\}_2Cr^I + 2\ C_6H_6 \xrightleftharpoons{\ AlCl_3\ } \{C_6H_6\}_2Cr^I + 2\ (CH_3)_3C_6H_3$$

Cyclic Condensation (H. Zeiss, W. Herwig)

Disubstituted acetylenes such as 2-butyne and tolane are smoothly trimerized at low temperatures by organometallic derivatives such as trimethyl- and triphenyl-chromium(III) to the arenes, hexamethyl- and hexaphenylbenzenes, respectively, and the corresponding arene π-complexes (92,148). Organo-manganese, -cobalt, -nickel, and -chromium(II) (128,129, 130) have also been used to promote the cyclic condensation of acetylenes. The yield of π-complex is generally lower than that of the free arene. The use of an acetylene with different substituents, e.g., $CH_3C \equiv CC_6H_5$, in the cyclization results in a statistical yield of arene product, namely, triphenylmesitylene and 1,3,4 - triphenyl - 2,5,6 - trimethylbenzene (151). Monosubstituted acetylenes may not be employed in cyclic condensation, since acetylenic hydrogen is sufficiently acidic to destroy the organometallic reagent.

Little has been done to clarify the course of the cyclization and π-complex formation, although it is pertinent to mention that organocobalt is a powerful catalyst in the cyclization of 2-butyne (130). The steady-state concentration of π-complex in this reaction suggests that it is acting as the catalytic center for condensation of the acetylene molecules.

Krüerke, Hoogzand, and Hübel (104) have provided a valuable piece of information by the isolation of a tert-butylacetylene-cobalt carbonyl intermediate, $[(CH_3)_3CC \equiv CH]_3Co_2(CO)_4$, and its subsequent decomposition with bromine to 1,2,4-tri-tert-butylbenzene. The molecular structure of this remarkable complex has now been determined by Mills and Robinson (110).

The phenomenon of hydrogen transfer by organochromium centers was mentioned in the previous section on Grignard Synthesis of π-complexes. This occurs also during cyclic condensation of acetylenes on organochromium, provided the hydrogen atom is in the immediate vicinity of the metal atom. The trimerization of 2-butyne or tolane on triphenylchromium(III) is accompanied, or may be dominated, by an intramolecular reaction between two molecules of the acetylene and one of the phenyl substituents, giving 1,2,3,4-tetramethyl- or 1,2,3,4-tetraphenyl-naphthalene (92). Trimethyl- or triethyl-chromium(III) and tolane leads to tetraphenylcyclopentadiene or 1,2,3,4-tetraphenylbenzene, respectively, in addition to the trimerization product (128). On the other hand, trimesitylchromium(III) or dimesityl-chromium(II) and these acetylenes give only arenes and arene π-complexes (129). Clearly, hydrogen is being transferred by chromium from the *ortho*-position of phenyl substituents and from methyl and ethyl groups in these syntheses.

In another variation Fischer, Müller, and Kuzel (52) have taken advantage of the hydrogen-abstracting property of organochromium in combining triethylchromium(III) with 1,3-cyclohexadiene. Bis-benzene-chromium is obtained in *ca.* 15% yield.

The remarkable power of organochromium as an oxidizing agent heavily weights this aspect of π-complex synthesis and deserves considerably more study.

Direct Route

One preparation of an arene π-complex by direct union of a transition metal and arene components has been reported (115). Metallic chromium and protonated toluene react to form the bis-toluene-chromium(I) cation. The direct route to arene π-complexes does not have wide applicability.

THE π-COMPLEXES (Table 2–I)

Titanium

Natta *et al.* (112) obtained a violet complex from the reaction of $TiCl_4/Al/AlCl_3/C_6H_6$ and formulated it as a σ-phenyl-aluminum compound, $TiCl_3 \cdot AlCl_3 \cdot AlCl_2C_6H_5$. The formulation has been challenged by Martin and Vohwinkel (109) and also by DeVries (23), who believe the substance to be an arene π-complex on the basis of its preparation (Fischer-Hafner conditions) and its chemical reactions. The correct equation of preparation and structure is claimed to be

$$3 C_6H_6 + 3 TiCl_4 + 2 Al + 4 AlCl_3 \rightarrow 3 \{C_6H_6\}TiCl_2 \cdot (AlCl_3)_2$$

One of the arguments advanced by the latter author in favor of the π-complex structure is that, whereas phenylaluminum dichloride is reduced relatively slowly by titanium tetrachloride with consequent formation of biphenyl, the complex in question is reduced instantaneously by the same reagent without a trace of biphenyl resulting. This would be the only recorded example of an arene-titanium π-complex.

Vanadium

Bis-benzene-vanadium(0) has been prepared both by the Fischer-Hafner process and by the reaction between phenyl Grignard and vanadium tetrachloride. Fischer and Kögler (44) formulate the aluminum method as involving first reduction and then disproportionation of the cation on hydrolysis:

$$VCl_4 + Al + 2 C_6H_6 \xrightarrow{AlCl_3} [\{C_6H_6\}_2V^I][AlCl_4]$$

$$5 \{C_6H_6\}_2V^I \rightarrow 4 \{C_6H_6\}_2V^0 + V^V + 2 C_6H_6$$

The black π-complex is oxidized at once by air to the brown-red cation. Bis-mesitylene-vanadium is also known both in the zerovalent and cationic state.

Chromium, Molybdenum, Tungsten

The best known of the arene π-complexes, bis-benzene-chromium was in fact prepared in 1919 by Hein (79). However, the extreme water-solubility of its cationic hydroxide and halides precluded its isolation, and it went undiscovered until 1955. However, its less soluble neighbors, bis-biphenyl-chromium(I) and biphenyl-benzene-chromium(I), were separated from the hydrolyzed Grignard product (cf. Grignard Synthesis section) and labeled as "tetraphenylchromium" and "triphenylchromium" cations, respectively. Later work on these organochromium products by Zeiss and Tsutsui, together with the structural proposal of Onsager (145), led to the correct formulation of the bis-arene π-complexes in 1954 and the subsequent isolation of the bis-benzene-chromium cation in the form of its tetraphenylboron salt (146,147).

Brown-black bis-benzene-chromium(0) and its yellow cation are best prepared by the Fischer-Hafner process (cf. the Aluminum Method section). Other arene derivatives such as bis-toluene-, -xylenes, -cumene, -tetralin, -mesitylene, -biphenyl, etc. are likewise readily accessible by this method. Cyclic condensation of acetylenes on organochromium has some advantage in the preparation of fully substituted arene complexes, but yields are generally low.

A mixed cyclopentadienyl-arene-chromium π-complex is reported to arise by synthesis from a $1:1$ mixture of Grignard reagents and chromium trichloride (45):

$$CrCl_3/C_5H_5MgBr/C_6H_5MgBr \xrightarrow[\text{2) } H_2O]{\text{1) } Et_2O} \{C_5H_5\}\{C_6H_6\}Cr^I$$

Arene π-complexes having substituted functional groups are very few. These are inaccessible by the aluminum route because of the $Al/AlCl_3$ conditions. However, carboxylation of the intermediate arising from reaction between phenyl Grignard and chromium(III) trichloride permits the isolation of the benzoic acid-biphenylchromium(I) cationic salt and the preparation of its methyl ester (14). Bis-benzoic acid-chromium is apparently completely unstable, since none could be isolated. However, it appears to exist as a barium salt (146). Fischer and Brunner (33,34,35) have metalated bis-benzene-chromium(0) with amylsodium and carbonated the resulting disodium product. However, the isolation of the free dicarboxylic acid failed, since they were obliged to esterify the disodium salt in order to obtain product. (Cf. Reactions of the π-Complexes.)

Green bis-benzene-molybdenum(0) and its cation are obtained in 70% yield by the aluminum method (56,61b). It is stated that the cation is formed first and that this then undergoes alkaline disproportionation:

$$6 \{C_6H_6\}_2Mo^+ + 8 \ OH^- \rightarrow 5 \ \{C_6H_6\}_2Mo^0 + MoO^{-2} + 4 \ H_2O + 2 \ C_6H_6$$

Bis-mesitylene-molybdenum is also preparable by this method both in the zerovalent and in the cationic form. The neutral complexes are even more sensitive toward oxidation by air than those of chromium.

A mixed cyclopentadienyl-arene π-complex of molybdenum is described as a red substance arising from the reduction of its carbonyl cation (46,47):

$$[\{C_5H_5\}\{C_6H_6\}(CO)Mo][PF_6] \xrightarrow[0^0]{LiAlH_4/THF} \{C_5H_5\}\{C_6H_6\}Mo^0$$

Yellow-green bis-benzene-tungsten(0) and its yellow cation have been synthesized from tungsten(VI) hexachloride by aluminum reduction but only in 2% yield (56). Alkaline disproportionation of the cation, forming the zerovalent complex and W(VI) similar to the equation above for the bis-benzene-molybdenum cation, is reported. Bis-benzene-tungsten(0) is somewhat less sensitive to air than its molybdenum counterpart. It is easily oxidized by iodine to the cationic salt:

$$2\{C_6H_6\}_2W^0 + I_2 \rightarrow 2[\{C_6H_6\}_2W^I]I$$

Manganese, Technetium, Rhenium

The sole bis-arene complex of manganese presently known was obtained by the cyclic condensation of 2-butyne on diphenylmanganese (130). The pink diamagnetic bis-hexamethylbenzene-manganese(I) cation was isolated in 11% yield as its tetraphenylboron salt. However, a mixed arene complex of manganese was obtained by Grignard synthesis from methyl-cyclopentadienyl-manganese chloride or bis-cyclopentadienyl-manganese (18,19):

$$(CH_3C_5H_4)_2Mn + C_6H_5MgBr \xrightarrow{THF} \xrightarrow{H_2O}$$
$$\{C_6H_6\}\{CH_3C_5H_4\}Mn + CH_3C_5H_5 + MgBrOH$$

The bis-benzene-technetium cation was formed by the normal Fischer-Hafner process (114):

$$TcCl_4 + Al + x \ AlCl_3 + 2 \ C_6H_6 \rightarrow [\{C_6H_6\}_2Tc] \cdot [AlCl_4] \cdot x \ AlCl_3,$$

and uniquely by neutron bombardment of bis-benzene-molybdenum(0) (4,5):

$$\{C_6H_6\}_2Mo \xrightarrow{n\gamma} \{C_6H_6\}_2^{99}Mo \xrightarrow{\beta^-} \{C_6H_6\}_2^{99m}Tc \longrightarrow {}^{99}Tc \cdots$$

Bis-benzene- and bis-mesitylene-π-complex cations of rhenium have been made by the aluminum method (62). The cations as well as those above of manganese and technetium are isoelectronic with the chromium(0) complex. Consequently, it is not surprising that these are not reduced (as is the bis-arene-chromium(I) cation) by dithionite ion or hypophosphorous acid.

Iron, Ruthenium, Osmium

The bis-arene iron complexes are obtained directly from the ferrous ion and arenes (30,31):

$$FeBr_2 + 2 \text{ Arene} \xrightarrow{AlCl_3} \{Arene\}_2Fe^{II}Br_2$$

The xylenes, mesitylene, durene, and hexamethylbenzene, form stable complex salts with iron. However, bis-benzene- and bis-toluene-iron(II) ions are quite susceptible to hydrolysis and must be isolated rapidly (127). Exchange of carbonyl ligands with arene is the basis for the preparation of the mixed cyclopentadienyl-mesitylene-iron iodide from cyclopentadienyl-dicarbonyl-iron dichloride (19):

$$\{C_5H_5\}(CO)_2Fe^{II}Cl_2 + (CH_3)_3C_6H_3 \xrightarrow[\text{2) } H_2O,\ KI]{\text{1) } AlCl_3} \{C_5H_5\}\{(CH_3)_3C_6H_3\}Fe^{II} + 2 \text{ CO}$$

The very stable orange bis-hexamethylbenzene-iron(II) cation (127) is reduced in a buffered solution of dithionite ion to the deep violet Fe^I complex (55). Complete reduction to the black, paramagnetic ($\uparrow\uparrow$), extremely sensitive (light, air, temperature) bis-hexamethylbenzene-iron(0) compound is possible in alkaline dithionite under pentane.

The Grignard method used previously for oxidizing 1,3-cyclohexadiene with chromium(III) chloride (52) has been applied with iron(III) chloride (50). The product is reported to be benzene-1,3-cyclohexadiene-iron(0).

The bis-mesitylene complexes of ruthenium and osmium are both prepared by the aluminum method from ruthenium(III) chloride and osmium(IV) chloride (60), e.g.,

$$3 \text{ RuCl}_3 + Al + 6 \text{ Arene} + 5 \text{ AlCl}_3 \rightarrow 3[\{Arene\}_2Ru^{II}][AlCl_4]_2$$

A new approach to π-complex synthesis is now described by Chatt and Robinson (16a). The reduction of *trans*-ruthenium(II) chloride by sodium-arenes (benzene, naphthalene, anthracene, and phenanthrene) appears to give a tautomeric mixture of hydrido-aryl and arene complexes, PP = $(CH_3)_2PCH_2CH_2P(CH_3)_2$:

$$\textit{trans-}(PP)_2Ru^{II}Cl_2 + 2 \text{ Na} \cdot C_{10}H_8 \rightarrow \{C_{10}H_8\}(PP)_2Ru^0 + 2 \text{ NaCl} + C_{10}H_8$$

$$\{C_{10}H_8\}(PP)_2Ru^0 \rightleftharpoons \textit{cis-}(C_{10}H_7)(PP)_2Ru^{II}H$$

Pyrolysis of the mixture gives naphthalene and a new mixture which on the basis of its physical properties and chemical behavior appears to be this:

$$(PP)_2Ru^0 \rightleftharpoons (PP)((CH_3)_2PCH_2CH_2P(CH_3)CH_2)Ru^{II}H$$

The internal transfer of hydrogen within complexes has been identified previously, as described earlier in the chapter, but these most recent examples are remarkable in that they show the ease by which hydrogen can move over metal centers.

Cobalt, Rhodium, Iridium

Bis-mesitylene-cobalt(III), -rhodium(III), and -iridium(III) were briefly mentioned some years ago as arising from the corresponding halides *via* the aluminum method. Apparently, these complexes are unstable and difficult to characterize, since no further details have become available in the meanwhile.

However, cobalt(II) chloride in molten hexamethylbenzene with aluminum chloride leads to the paramagnetic ($\uparrow$) cobalt(II) complex (48):

$$CoCl_2 + 2\ AlCl_3 + 2(CH_3)_6C_6 \rightarrow [\{(CH_3)_6C_6\}_2Co^{II}][AlCl_4]_2$$

The ion is thus isoelectronic with the corresponding Fe^I complex. The former undergoes facile disproportionation in neutral or strongly acid solution to the bis-arene-Co^I and, as formulated, the bis-arene-Co^{III} cations. The latter could not be isolated:

$$2[\{(CH_3)_6C_6\}_2Co^{II}]^{2+} \rightarrow [\{(CH_3)_6C_6\}_2Co^I]^+ + [\{(CH_3)_6C_6\}_2Co^{III}]^{3+}$$

A more direct route to the bis-arene-cobalt(I) ion was found simply by adding a stoichiometric amount of aluminum to the original reaction mixture. The yellow, paramagnetic ($\uparrow\uparrow$) bis-hexamethylbenzene-cobalt(I) ion was isolated in the form of a variety of salts:

$$3\ CoCl_2 + Al + 3\ AlCl_3 + 6\ (CH_3)_6C_6 \rightarrow 3[\{(CH_3)_3C_6\}_2Co^I][AlCl_4]$$

This ion is isoelectronic with the corresponding Fe^0 complex.

Here a discrepancy arises. The bis-hexamethylbenzene-cobalt(I) ion was prepared earlier by the condensation of diphenylacetylene on dimesityl-cobalt(II), but this we reported to be deep red and diamagnetic (130). Clearly, the two substances are dissimilar. The chemical and analytical evidence for the identity of our complex is consistent, but the physical properties point in another direction. The problem and its peculiarities stand unresolved.

The bis-arene cobalt(I) and (II) ions prepared by Fischer and Lindner can be reduced to paramagnetic ($\uparrow$) bis-hexamethylbenzene-cobalt(0) in liquid ammonia with sodium (49):

$$[\{(CH_3)_6C_6\}_2Co^I][PF_6] + Na \rightarrow \{(CH_3)_6C_6\}_2Co^0 + NaPF_6$$

It is to be noted in particular that the dipole moment of this zerovalent complex is 1.78 ± 0.07 D, excluding the centrosymmetric structure of bis-benzene-chromium(0). The several apparent anomalies associated with the cobalt(II, I, 0) arene complexes, namely excess of orbital electrons over the krypton number of 36, and unusual properties, are certain to attract considerable attention to this element in future work.

Similar complexes of bis-hexamethylbenzene-rhodium and -iridium are also preparable by methods similar to those just described for cobalt (48,49).

However, attempts to prepare the bis-benzene π-complexes of these metals have failed.

The mixed benzene-cyclopentadienyl-cobalt(III) cation has been synthesized from cyclopentadienyl-1,3-hexadiene-cobalt(I) by abstraction of hydrogen with triphenylmethyl tetrafluoborate (36).

REACTIONS OF THE π-COMPLEXES

Substitution (Metalation)

The chemistry of the metallocenes, $e.g.$, bis-cyclopentadienyl-iron(II), and the metallarenes is readily distinguished by the susceptibility of the former and the resistance of the latter to nucleophilic, electrophilic, and radical reactions (145). However, Fischer and Brunner were at last able to metalate bis-benzene-chromium(0) with amylsodium (33,34,35). The reaction is not facile, the products are mixed, and the yields are generally low:

$$\{C_{12}H_{12}\}Cr^0 + n\ C_5H_{11}Na \rightarrow \{C_{12}H_{12-n}Na_n\}Cr^0 + n\ C_5H_{12}$$

Metalation is not clean, as shown by treatment of the reaction mixture with methyl iodide and subsequent decomposition to benzene, toluene, m- and p-xylene, together with lesser amounts of o-xylene and trimethylbenzenes. Carbonation and esterification gave π-complexes containing one, two, three, and even four carbomethoxy groups distributed throughout the rings. Reaction with formaldehyde or acetaldehyde led to benzyl alcohol and secondary alcohol complexes, respectively; whereas benzaldehyde gave rise to benzene-benzophenone-chromium(0). On the other hand, metalated bis-benzene-chromium(0) and benzophenone produced benzene-triphenylcarbinol complexes.

One attempted Friedel-Crafts acylation of the arene ring in benzene-cyclopentadienyl-chromium(I) and -manganese(I) quite surprisingly caused ring enlargement to cyclopentadienyl-methylcycloheptatrienyl-chromium(I) and -manganese(I) (32).

Oxidation-Reduction

The preparative methods for obtaining the arene π-complexes in various degrees of oxidation have been described in previous sections. However, additional ones involve the use of hydrogen chloride (85) and alkyl halides (116). In both cases, bis-arene-chromium(0) complexes are oxidized, giving the bis-arene-chromium(I) ion and hydrogen in the first, hydrocarbons in the second. Aluminum chloride is also said to oxidize bis-arene complexes of chromium(0) to (I) (83):

$$3\{Arene\}_2Cr^0 + 4\ AlCl_3 \rightarrow 3[\{Arene\}_2Cr^I][AlCl_4] + Al^0$$

Bis-benzene-chromium(0) has also been oxidized with di-tert-butylperoxide to tetra-tert-butoxychromium(IV) (75,3).

Disproportionation of the bis-biphenyl-chromium(I) cation is stated to occur when an aqueous or methanolic solution is either heated or irradiated. Bis-biphenyl-chromium(0) is formed and the oxidation product, chromium(II) ion, may be captured with 2,2'-dipyridyl (91).

Arene Exchange

The exchange reactions of arene π-complexes are by far the most important at this date. Their readiness to exchange arene rings for carbon monoxide is now well established, and this subject is discussed in detail in Chapter 3. However, arenes exchange also, and this has had a role in simplifying the aluminum preparative procedure described previously.

Hein and Kartte have carried out a series of arene exchanges with bis-arene-chromium(0) complexes. Displacement of the hydrocarbons, benzene, biphenyl, mesitylene, tetralin and p,p'-ditolyl, is catalyzed by aluminum chloride, and the equilibria are subject to the normal effects of concentration of the reaction components (82).

Catalysis

Ethylene has been polymerized with bis-arene chromium. Highly linear polyethylene has been made with bis-benzene-chromium(0) as catalyst in the presence of a trace of oxygen (144). Another catalytic system consisting of bis-arene-chromium and a trialkyl or dialkylaluminum has been used also (72).

Dimesitylcobalt(II) trimerizes 2-butyne to hexamethylbenzene, presumably via π-complex, with a catalytic efficiency which increases with acetylene concentration (130). The anomalies associated with the arene cobalt complexes already mentioned undoubtedly are intimately related to their catalytic activity.

π-Complexes are also claimed to be intermediates in hydrogenation processes (137).

PHYSICAL PROPERTIES

Compounds which possess at the time of their discovery unrecognized types of chemical bonding promote the search for physicochemical evidence which leads to and supports new concepts of bonding. Several empirical and theoretical treatments of the bond properties of bis-arene-metal complexes have appeared, ranging from fixed Kekulé structures with three coordinate covalent bonds to the metal (39,120) to a variety of molecular orbital treatments. The interested reader is referred to Chapter 1 and to references 11, 12, 13, 25, 63, 107, 108, 119, 122, and 135 for detailed treatments.

Magnetic Properties

Early studies showed satisfactory agreement between the magnetic moment observed for a given complex and that predicted by the application of the "golden rule" of the noble (inert) gas configuration to stable complexes of the bis-arene-metals(0 or I) (41,53). Diamagnetism is observed with complexes in which the metal contains six electrons in the three d-orbitals remaining after d^2sp^3-hybridization. Accordingly, the bis-arene complexes or complex ions of the following metals are diamagnetic: neutral group VIA metals; mono-, di-, and trivalent metal complexes of the group VIIA and group VIII metals. Paramagnetism is observed with neutral or ionic complexes of metals having an uneven number of electrons (53):

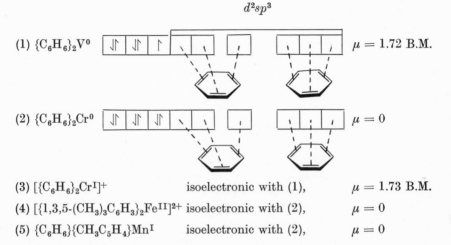

$$d^2sp^3$$

(1) $\{C_6H_6\}_2V^0$ $\mu = 1.72$ B.M.

(2) $\{C_6H_6\}_2Cr^0$ $\mu = 0$

(3) $[\{C_6H_6\}_2Cr^I]^+$ isoelectronic with (1), $\mu = 1.73$ B.M.

(4) $[\{1,3,5\text{-}(CH_3)_3C_6H_3\}_2Fe^{II}]^{2+}$ isoelectronic with (2), $\mu = 0$

(5) $\{C_6H_6\}\{CH_3C_5H_4\}Mn^I$ isoelectronic with (2), $\mu = 0$

Mixed arene-cyclopentadienyl and arene-tropylium complexes also adhere to this scheme. However, the bis-hexamethylbenzene-cobalt(I) cation is one of the exceptions since it contains two more electrons than can be accommodated in the remaining three $3d$ orbitals. This complex cation is reported to have a magnetic moment of 2.95 B.M. corresponding to two unpaired electrons (48), while the bis-arene-cobalt(II) di-cation has only one unpaired electron.

Another complex to which the bis-hexamethylbenzene-cobalt(I) structure was assigned is found to be diamagnetic (130). This discrepancy in identity and properties remains a source of interest.

A correlation between a molecular orbital model of bis-cyclopentadienyl- and bis-arene-metal complexes and their magnetic moments has been made (122).

Dipole Moments

Bis-benzene-chromium(0) as well as bis-toluene-chromium(0) and the isomeric bis-xylene-chromium(0) complexes have no detectable dipole moments ($0 \pm 0.35 - 0.48$ D) indicating a *trans*-configuration of substituents (58,138):

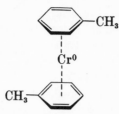

Curious and unexplained is the observation, however, that bis-(methyl benzoate)-chromium(0) has a moment of 2.49 ± 0.05 D (33). This compound was prepared *via* metalation by amylsodium followed by carboxylation and esterification. The possibility of partial di-metalation of one arene cannot be excluded on basis of the evidence presented.

Electrochemistry

The ease with which oxidation of bis-arene-chromium(0) occurs has led to the study of the redox process by polarographic techniques (68,69,100, 134,135,138). The system is reversible since the same position (−0.81 V *vs.* 0.2 N calomel) of the half-wave potential is found irrespective of whether it is approached from the oxidized or the reduced species (68):

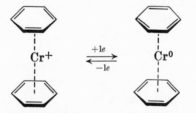

The oxidized state can readily be prepared by air oxidation of the neutral species, and if polarograms are taken during the oxidation, it is possible to detect both oxidation and reduction waves simultaneously. Equimolar mixtures of A and B gave two separate steps to the same height. This observation of equal diffusion coefficient coupled with proportionality between diffusion current and concentration allows the calculation of the magnitude of the diffusion current from Ilkovič's equation. Although a complete electromotive series is not known in the solvent mixture used (methanol-benzene), it is significant, in relation to the stability of transition metal ions in low valence states, that the bis-arene-chromium(I) cation is less readily reduced than the Zn^{2+} and more readily than the Cd^{2+} ion. Comparison between the half-wave potential of variously substituted bis-arene-chromium species reveals a stepwise increase to more negative potentials per methyl substituent (*i.e.* increased difficulty in reduction for electron donating substituents) and conversely a decrease for phenyl substituents (69,100,101,102). Similar results were obtained in dimethylformamide (96).

A more detailed study of the polarographic reduction wave of the bis-ethylbenzene-chromium system showed that in dilute solutions only one wave appears, but in more concentrated solutions two waves are detectable. This is interpreted in terms of separate reduction steps for adsorbed and non-adsorbed cationic complexes (134).

The interpretation of the electrochemical observations with respect to the much-discussed bonding forces in bis-arene-metal complexes led to the interesting conclusion (121,135,136) that the localization of the highest occupied orbitals could be derived from the oxidation potential and that of the lowest unoccupied orbitals from the reduction potential of the bis-arene-metal(0) complex. Application of this approach to a series of substituted bis-arene-chromium compounds revealed a parallelism in direction of the substitutional effect on the aromatic nucleus, whether bonded to a metal or not (although much less pronounced in the complexes). It was concluded that the highest occupied orbital is a bonding one; and more significantly, this orbital is mainly localized at the central atom. It was even estimated that the bonding orbital is localized, at most, to the extent of 10–15% near the rings, and the remainder at the central metal atom.

Thermodynamic Properties

The standard enthalpy of formation of bis-arene-metal(0) complexes has been evaluated by the heat-of-combustion method. The heat of combustion of bis-benzene-chromium(0) was determined to be 1723.7 ± 1.4 kcal/mole at $20°$ (57), while another group independently found -1696 ± 8 kcal/mole for ΔH_{298}° (29), the standard enthalpy of combustion:

$$\{C_6H_6\}_2Cr(s) + 15.75\ O_2(g) \rightarrow \tfrac{1}{2}\ Cr_2O_3(s) + 12\ CO_2(g) + 6\ H_2O(l)$$

By normal thermodynamic procedures the standard heat of formation was calculated by subtracting the heat of combustion from a summation of the standard heats of formation of $\tfrac{1}{2}\ Cr_2O_3(s)$, $6\ H_2O(l)$ and $12\ CO_2(g)$, giving $H_{293} = +51$ kcal/mole (57) and $\Delta H_{f\,298}^{\circ} = 21 \pm 8$ kcal (29). The heat of formation of bis-benzene-chromium(0) from its components was calculated from the independently determined vapor pressure and heat of sublimation of bis-benzene-chromium(0) (20) and also the standard heat of formation of benzene(l):

$$2\ C_6H_6(g) + Cr(g) \rightarrow \{C_6H_6\}_2Cr(g) \qquad H_{293} = -58.3\ \text{kcal/mole}$$

Comparable values calculated by two independent groups (excluding the heat of sublimation) were -99 kcal/mole (57) and -58.3 kcal/mole (29). When these values are compared with those for ferrocene, $H_{298} = -147$ kcal/mole, reasonable agreement between the relative stabilities is apparent. Separate determination of the enthalpies of formation of bis-benzene-chromium(0), bis-(1,3,5-trimethylbenzene)-chromium(0) and bis-(1,2,4-trimethylbenzene)-chromium(0) from chromium(g) and the hydrocarbons by analogous procedures (59) showed the apparent higher stability of the methyl-substituted bis-arene-chromium(0) complexes compared to bis-benzene-chromium(0) by *ca.* 20 kcal/mole. That no difference is found between the two trimethyl-substituted benzene isomers is yet another indication of the lack of added stability in arene complexes of pronounced three-fold symmetry.

Comparison between the bis-benzene-chromium(0), -molybdenum(0), and -vanadium(0) complexes (54) led to the result that the standard enthalpy changes of formation of these complexes from gaseous benzene and the metal increase in the order: -56.6 (Cr); -101.9 (Mo); and -143.4 (V). In enthalpy changes, however, lie hidden terms which may differ from complex to complex, namely the excitation energy for the metal and the benzene molecules (the former have been estimated to be 185 and 133 kcal/mole for $\{C_6H_6\}_2Cr$ and $\{C_6H_6\}_2Mo$, respectively (122)).

Spectra

Infrared. Much effort has been spent in normal coordinate analyses of the infrared and Raman spectra of bis-arene-metals(0 or I). The problem is challenging inasmuch as the infrared spectrum of benzene itself is understood in detail. It was hoped that evidence concerning the symmetry of the benzene ligand would lend support to one of the existing bonding theories. This objective appeared achievable since the opposing schools of thought favored either D_{3d} or D_{6h} symmetry (64). Prior to a major publication on the subject (66) results had been communicated which predicted D_{3d} symmetry for neutral $\{C_6H_6\}_2Cr^0$ (65,67). An independent group of workers (124) had assigned the absorption bands of crystalline $\{C_6H_6\}_2Cr$ and $\{C_6D_6\}_2Cr$ differently and had arrived at the conclusion that six-fold symmetry was present.

The more extensive study (66) is mainly concerned with the interpretation of the spectrum of the cationic complex $\{C_6H_6\}_2Cr^+$. A symmetry determination for the structure of the ligands was made under premises of coupled vibration and the presence of a center of symmetry. For the purpose of the discussion the following symmetry groups for the single ligands were considered: D_{6h}, C_{6v}, D_{3h}, D_{3d}, and C_{3v}. However, on the basis of the presence of an inversion center the complex as a whole can have only D_{6h} and D_{3d} symmetry. This leaves D_{6h}, D_{3d}, and D_{3h} as possible symmetries for the ligands. A stepwise analysis of the infrared and Raman spectra led to the conclusion that, within the limitations of the vibrational spectra, the cationic complex $\{C_6H_6\}_2Cr^+$ possesses D_{6h} symmetry. The same symmetry was derived for $\{C_6H_6\}_2V^0$ (38) and perhaps holds also for the molybdenum(0) and tungsten(0) complexes. However, the total symmetry D_{3d} and the local ligand symmetry D_{3h} were derived for the neutral chromium complex. The latter conclusion, which was supported by the same authors in a recent review article (64), is in disagreement with the refined structure determination by X-ray crystallographic methods (21,97; for a discussion of the data, see Chapter 1). The repeated reversals of opinions on the symmetry properties of bis-benzene-chromium(0), as derived from normal coordinate analyses originating from one group, is an outstanding example of the weaknesses inherent in the method. Recently a thorough electron diffraction analysis of bis-benzene-chromium(0) in the gas phase revealed the higher order of symmetry, D_{6h} (73a). The C—C bond distances in the regular hexagonal benzene ligands were 1.423 $\pm$ 0.002 Å. Particular efforts were taken to detect distortion of the benzene rings, but none was found.

For identification purposes the following spectral regions are of significance (37): The normal skeletal vibrations appear at lower wave numbers when the benzenoid compound is present as a π-bonded ligand. The "1600 band" appears at 1430–1410 cm^{-1} and the "1500 band" at 1140–1120 cm^{-1}; in addition, two to three deformation modes appear in the 1000–995 cm^{-1} region and one or two between 790 and 740 cm^{-1}. In the far infrared region two bands appear between 490 and 330 cm^{-1}, one of which has been assigned to a metal-ring valence vibration.

Visible and Ultraviolet Spectra. It is curious that although the colors of bis-arene-metal(0) or metal(I) complexes are often mentioned, no systematic study of the *visible spectra* of a series of these complexes has appeared. Relative to the bonding of such complexes, the *ultraviolet spectra* are perhaps more elucidating. The first report listed six bands for the ultraviolet spectrum of the bis-benzene-chromium(I) cation (143), three of which were found near the positions of three bands in the spectra of arene-tricarbonyl-chromium(0) complexes. The long-wave length bands for the cationic complex corresponded to the normal bands of chromium(I) complexes (27,142). In the ultraviolet region six and seven bands have been reported for solution spectra of bis-benzene-chromium(0) and bis-benzene-chromium(I), respectively (141,143). More fine structure was expected from vapor spectra of bis-benzene-chromium(0) (9). Indeed the vapor spectrum was dramatically different from the solution spectra. Three main band systems aside from other less distinct bands with superimposed vibrational structure were clearly distinguished at 374.8 mμ, 305.0 mμ and in the range 282.0–267.0 mμ (a system of three groups).

The assignment of these bands was made on basis of D_{6h} symmetry, and lent considerable support to some of the various energy-level diagrams calculated by molecular orbital schemes (8,106,123). It was concluded that the experimental results coupled with arguments involved in the assignment of transitions gave stronger evidence for the presence of a regular hexagonal benzene ligand than for one of D_{3d} symmetry.

X-ray K-band Spectra. Absorption spectra in the X-ray K-band region have been recorded for a number of complexes (10,42,133). The conclusions reached in the interpretation of these spectra in the most recent series of papers have been energetically refuted (2). The method would be of considerable interest if it allowed unequivocal conclusions concerning the effective charge on the central atom and on the ligand in complexes. However, the calculation of results in this application to bis-arene complexes is disputed, and the development of the extended method of calculation of the effective charge both at central atom and at the ligands can only be anticipated.

Certain irregularities in expected parallelisms between the heats of formation of some arene-π-complexes and their retention values in the Szilard-Chalmers process have been recorded (6).

Electron Spin Resonance. Electron spin resonance spectra of the bis-benzene-chromium(I), -molybdenum(I), and -tungsten(I) cations have been reported (26,28,76,77,78,118), as have those of bis-biphenyl-chromium(I) (131) and bis-benzene-vanadium(0) (78). For the complexes the magnetic moment measurement had shown the presence of one unpaired electron. At proper dilutions the aqueous solutions of both bis-benzene-chromium(I) and bis-biphenyl-chromium(I) ions show hyperfine splitting which indicates interaction of the protons on the arene with the unpaired electron (midpoint g = 1.9863). The detection of 11 poorly separated lines in the former and 8 in the latter ion is significant (13 and 12, respectively, would be expected from 12 and 10 equivalent protons). Thus, a clear indication of interaction between an even and an uneven number of protons, respectively, on the benzenoid compound linked to the metal is found. The mechanism of this remarkable interaction, however, is defined only by "explaining" these observations as a deep-seated hybridization or "Wechselwirkung" of the π-orbitals of the rings and the d-orbitals of the central atom. In very high resolution of hyperfine proton splitting, the additional splitting by ^{53}Cr (having $I = \frac{3}{2}$) can be detected (76).

Bis-benzene-vanadium(0), vanadium having a nuclear spin quantum number of $\frac{7}{2}$, shows the proper eight-line fundamental pattern (g = 1.9624) in which the proton-splitting in each of these lines can be perceived (78). From a comparison of the coupling constant between the unpaired electron and the ring proton in bis-benzene-chromium(0) ($\langle Cr \rangle_p$ 3.25 gauss) and bis-benzene-vanadium(0) ($\langle V \rangle_p$ 4.0) it was concluded that the unpaired electron is more closely associated with the central atom in the chromium complex than in the vanadium complex where it spends a somewhat longer time in both rings. This is intuitively reasonable since for electrostatic reasons one would expect in these two isoelectronic complexes that the chromium(I) of charge +1 would favor less separation of the unpaired electron from the metal atom than that found in the uncharged vanadium(0) complex.

Bis-arene-metal complexes of chromium(I), molybdenum(I), and tungsten(I) are particularly well suited for studying the temperature dependence of relaxation processes, which in the electron spin resonance spectrum influences the line width of the hyperfine splitting (78). This is due to extensive spin-orbit coupling in these complexes. These complexes which, aside from their inner-sphere electrons, are isoelectronic show a regular increase both in the shift of the g-value from the positions for the free electron and in the anisotropy of the g-value with increasing atomic number of the central metal atom.

The solution spectrum for bis-benzene-chromium(I) undergoes first a line sharpening; then at −100° a transition appears in which the hyperfine splitting is smeared out. Finally at still lower temperatures, when the solvent becomes very viscous, resolution due to direct magnetic dipole coupling becomes recognizable. The molybdenum complex shows a similar effect although hyperfine splitting is not observed at room temperature. The tungsten complex, on the other hand, gives no signal at room temperature and only a poorly resolved one at lower temperatures (78).

Evidence for the presence in solution of a new type of charge-transfer complex between vanadium oxide chloride and aromatic compounds has recently been derived from electron spin-resonance measurements (103).

Nuclear Magnetic Resonance. Nuclear magnetic resonance has not been used extensively in the study of π-arene complexes partly because of the inherent difficulties involved in observing spectra of paramagnetic complexes and partly because of the limited solubility of the complexes. Most spectra recorded are those of mixed, cyclopentadienyl- or cyclohexadienyl-arene-metal complexes (32,99). These spectra are best discussed in relation to arene-carbonyl-metal complexes in Chapter 3 because of a revision in the assignments of the proton signals.

Evidence has been obtained from nuclear magnetic studies showing that the benzene molecule in the benzene-silver perchlorate complex rotates around the molecular axis (70). See page 5.

In general it appears that the protons of the arene π-bonded to a transition metal give a resonance signal which is shifted toward higher fields as compared to the free arene molecule. This is consistent with the partial shielding of the protons by removal of the deshielding effect of the π-electrons as the electrons become involved in π-bonding to the transition metal. The shift has been measured to be 2.93 ppm toward higher field relative to free benzene (1). The line narrowing which is as pronounced in bis-benzene-chromium as in ferrocene has been interpreted to be associated with internal molecular rotation of the benzene molecule (111). This motion could be frozen out at −196° as seen by a pronounced broadening of the resonance signal. An argument based on the line width of the proton signal leads to the same conclusion for bis-benzene-chromium(III).

TABLE 2–I

π-Arene-Metal Complexes

Formula	M.P. (°C)	Reference (Chapter 2)
{Arene}$_2$M^0		
{C$_6$H$_6$}$_2$V^0	277–278	44, 105
{1,3,5-(CH$_3$)$_3$C$_6$H$_3$}$_2$V^0	126–127	16
{C$_6$H$_6$}$_2$Cr^0	284–285	39, 40, 60, 93, 138, 147
{C$_6$H$_5$D}$_2$Cr^0	282–284	33, 147
{CH$_3$C$_6$H$_5$}$_2$Cr^0		53, 139
{C$_6$H$_5$C$_2$H$_5$}$_2$Cr^0		134
{C$_6$H$_5$COOCH$_3$}$_2$Cr^0	106–108	33, 34, 35
{1,3,5-(CH$_3$)$_3$C$_6$H$_3$}$_2$Cr^0		53, 60
{C$_{12}$H$_{12}$}$_2$Cr^0 tetralin		53
{(C$_6$H$_5$)$_2$}$_2$Cr^0	112	61a, 150
{4-ClC$_6$H$_4$C$_6$H$_5$}$_2$Cr^0	105–108	15
{(CH$_3$)$_6$C$_6$}$_2$Cr^0		53, 140
{1,2,3,4-(C$_6$H$_5$)$_4$C$_4$H$_6$}Cr^0 tetraphenylbutane	145–146	126
{(CH$_3$)$_6$C$_6$}$_2$Fe^0		55
{(CH$_3$)$_6$C$_6$}$_2$Co^0	115	49
{C$_6$H$_6$}$_2$Mo^0	115d	56, 61b
{1,3,5-(CH$_3$)$_3$C$_6$H$_3$}$_2$Ru^0		53
{C$_6$H$_6$}$_2$W^0	160d	56
{C$_6$H$_6$}{C$_5$H$_4$CH$_3$}Mn^{I}		19
[{C$_6$H$_6$}{C$_5$H$_5$}Fe^{II}]$^+$Br$_3$$^-$		73
[{C$_6$H$_6$}{C$_5$H$_5$}Fe^{II}]$^+$[AlCl$_4$]$^-$		113
[{C$_6$H$_6$}{C$_5$H$_5$}Fe^{II}]$^+$[(C$_6$H$_5$)$_4$B]$^-$		113
{C$_6$H$_6$}{C$_5$H$_5$D}Fe^0		73, 99
{C$_6$H$_6$}{C$_6$H$_8$}Fe^0		50
[{1,3,5-(CH$_3$)$_3$C$_6$H$_3$}{C$_5$H$_5$}Fe^{II}]$^+$Br$_3$$^-$		73
[{1,3,5-(CH$_3$)$_3$C$_6$H$_3$}{C$_5$H$_5$}Fe^{II}]I$^-$		19
[{1,3,5-(CH$_3$)$_3$C$_6$H$_3$}{C$_5$H$_5$}Fe^{II}]$^+$[(C$_6$H$_5$)$_4$B]$^-$		113
[{1,3,5-(CH$_3$)$_3$C$_6$H$_3$}{C$_2$H$_5$C$_5$H$_4$}Fe^{II}]$^+$[(C$_6$H$_5$)$_4$B]$^-$	246.5	113
[{1,3,5-(CH$_3$)$_3$C$_6$H$_3$}{CH$_3$COC$_5$H$_4$}Fe^{II}]$^-$[(C$_6$H$_5$)$_4$B]$^-$	197–198	113
[{C$_{12}$H$_{12}$}{C$_5$H$_5$}Fe^{II}]$^+$[(C$_6$H$_5$)$_4$B]$^-$		113
[{C$_6$H$_6$}{C$_5$H$_5$}Co^{III}]$^{2+}$(PF$_6$)$_2$$^{2-}$		36
{C$_6$H$_6$}{C$_5$H$_5$}Mo^{I}	216–218	47
[{C$_6$H$_6$}{C$_5$H$_5$}Mo^{II}(CO)]$^+$PF$_6$$^-$		46
{C$_6$H$_6$}{C$_6$H$_8$}Ru^0	140d	51, 98
{(CF$_3$)$_6$C$_6$}{C$_5$H$_5$}Rh^{I}	185	24
[{1,3,5-(CH$_3$)$_3$C$_6$H$_3$}{C$_5$H$_5$}W(CO)]$^+$PF$_6$$^-$	145	46
{C$_6$H$_6$}{C$_6$H$_7$}Re^{I}	195	62, 98
{C$_6$H$_6$}{C$_6$H$_8$}Os^0	114–116	51
[{C$_6$H$_6$}Cu^{I}]$^+$[AlCl$_4$]$^-$		132
{Arene$_1$}{Arene$_2$}M^0		
{C$_6$H$_6$}{C$_6$H$_5$CHO}Cr^0	100–101	35
{C$_6$H$_6$}{C$_6$H$_5$CH$_2$OH}Cr^0		35
{C$_6$H$_6$}{C$_6$H$_5$COCH$_3$}Cr^0	111–112.5	35
{C$_6$H$_6$}{C$_6$H$_5$CH(OH)CH$_3$}Cr^0	80	35
{C$_6$H$_6$}{C$_6$H$_5$COOCH$_3$}Cr^0	82–83	34, 35

TABLE 2–I (continued)

Formula	M.P. (°C)	Reference (Chapter 2)
$\{C_6H_6\}\{(C_6H_5)_2\}Cr^0$	120–121	87
$\{C_6H_6\}\{(C_6H_5)_2CO\}Cr^0$	96.5–98	34
$\{C_6H_6\}\{(C_6H_5)_2CHOH\}Cr^0$	130–131	35
$\{C_6H_6\}\{(C_6H_5)_3COH\}Cr^0$	157.5	35
$\{Arene\}_2M^n$ (n = I, II, III)		
$[\{1,3,5\text{-}(CH_3)_3C_6H_3\}_2V^I]^+I^-$		16
$[\{1,3,5\text{-}(CH_3)_3C_6H_3\}_2V^I]^+[AlCl_4]^-$		44
$[\{1,3,5\text{-}(CH_3)_3C_6H_3\}_2V^I][V^{-I}(CO)_6]$	160–165	16
$[\{C_6H_6\}_2Cr^I]^+I^-$		40, 80, 82, 87
$[\{C_6H_6\}_2Cr^I]^+[AlCl_4]^-$		53
$[\{C_6H_6\}_2Cr^I]_2^{2+}Cr_2O_7^{2-}$		144
$[\{C_6H_6\}_2Cr^I]^+picrate^-$	138 expl.	39, 40, 53
$[\{C_6H_6\}_2Cr^I]^+[(C_6H_5)_4B]^-$		93, 147
$[[\{C_6H_6\}Cr^I]^+[\{C_5H_5\}Cr^0(CO)_3]^-$	215–216d	43
$[\{1,3,5\text{-}(CH_3)_3C_6H_3\}_2Cr^I]^+I^-$		82
$[\{(C_6H_5)_2\}_2Cr^I]^+Cl^-$		84, 91
$[\{(C_6H_5)_2\}_2Cr^I]^+I^-$	177–178	53, 61a, 82, 87, 117, 149, 150
$[\{(C_6H_5)_2\}_2Cr^I]^+OH^-$		91
$[\{(C_6H_5)_2\}_2Cr^I]^+[AlCl_4]^-$		83, 90
$[\{(C_6H_5)_2\}_2Cr^I]^+[HgCl_3]^-$		81
$[\{(C_6H_5)_2\}_2Cr^I]^+[Cr^{II}Cl_3]^-$		85
$[\{(C_6H_5)_2\}_2Cr^I]^+[Cr^{III}(CNS)_4(NH_3)_2]^-$	165–171	81
$[\{(C_6H_5)_2\}_2Cr^I]^+[Fe_4(CO)_{13}]^-$		90
$[\{(C_6H_5)_2\}_2Cr^I]^+[Co(CO)_4]^-$	84	86
$[\{(C_6H_5)_2\}_2Cr^I]^+[C_6H_5O]^-$	102–104	150
$[\{(C_6H_5)_2\}_2Cr^I]^+[(C_6H_5)_4B]^-$		82, 147
$[\{p\text{-}ClC_6H_4C_6H_5\}_2Cr^I]^+[(C_6H_5)_4B]^-$	200–202	15, 88
$[\{C_{12}H_{19}\}_2Cr^I]^+I^-$		53, 82
$[\{C_{12}H_{12}\}_2Cr^I]^+[picrate]^-$		53
$[\{(p\text{-}CH_3C_6H_4)_2\}_2Cr^I]^+I^-$		82
$[\{1,2,3,4\text{-}(C_6H_5)_4C_4H_6\}Cr^I]^+I^-$ tetraphenylbutane	145–146	126
$[\{(CH_3)_6C_6\}_2Mn^I]^+[(C_6H_5)_4B]^-$		130
$[\{1,3,5\text{-}(CH_3)_3C_6H_3\}_2Fe^{II}]^{2+}I_2^{2-}$		30
$\{1,3,5\text{-}(CH_3)_3C_6H_3\}_2FeAl_{2\cdot67}Br_{10}$		115
$[\{1,3,5\text{-}(CH_3)_3C_6H_3\}_2Fe^{II}]^{2+}[(C_6H_5)_4B]_2^{2-}$		30, 53
$[\{(CH_3)_6C_6\}_2Fe^I]^+[PF_6]^-$		55
$[\{1,3,5\text{-}(CH_3)_3C_6H_3\}_2Fe^{II}]^{2+}[Cr^{III}(SCN)_4(NH_3)_2]_2^{2-}$		30, 53
$[\{(CH_3)_6C_6\}_2Co^I]^+[PF_6]^-$	170d	48
$[\{(CH_3)_6C_6\}_2Co^{II}]^{2+}[PF_6]_2^-$	140d	48
$[\{(CH_3)_6C_6\}_2Co^{II}]^{2+}[PtCl_6]^{2-}$		37, 48
$[\{(CH_3)_6C_6\}_2Co^I]^+[(C_6H_5)_4B]^-$	210d	55, 130
$[\{C_6H_6\}_2Mo^I]^+I^-$		56
$[\{C_6H_6\}_2Mo^I]^+[\{C_5H_5\}Mo(CO)_3]^-$		30
$\{C_6H_5COO^-\}_2Mo^{II}$		1
$\{p\text{-}CH_3OC_6H_4COO^-\}_2Mo^{II}$		1
$\{o\text{-}CH_3C_6H_4COO^-\}_2Mo^{II}$		1
$[\{C_6H_6\}_2Tc^I]^+[PF_6]^-$	250d	4, 5, 114
$[\{C_6H_6\}_2Ru^{II}]^{2+}(ClO_4)_2^{2-}$		98
$[\{1,3,5\text{-}(CH_3)_3C_6H_3\}_2Ru^{II}]^{2+}(PF_6)_2^{2-}$		31

TABLE 2–I (continued)

Formula	M.P. (°C)	Reference (Chapter 2)
$[\{1,3,5\text{-}(CH_3)_3C_6H_3\}_2Ru^{II}]^{2+}[(C_6H_5)_4B]_2{}^{2-}$		31
$[\{(CH_3)_6C_6\}_2Rh^I]^+[PF_6]^-$	180d	37, 48
$[\{(CH_3)_6C_6\}_2Rh^{II}]^{2+}[PF_6]_2{}^{2-}$		48
$[\{(CH_3)_6C_6\}_2Rh^{II}]^{2+}[PtCl_6]^{2-}$		48
$[\{C_6H_6\}_2W^I]^+I^-$	.	56
$[\{1,3,5\text{-}(CH_3)_3C_6H_3\}_2Re^I]^+[Cr^{III}(SCN)_4(NH_3)_2]^-$		62
$[\{C_6H_6\}_2Re^I]^+[(C_6H_5)_4B]^-$		62
$[\{1,3,5\text{-}(CH_3)_3C_6H_3\}_2Os^{II}]^{2+}[(C_6H_5)_4B]_2{}^{2-}$		37
$[\{1,3,5\text{-}(CH_3)_3C_6H_3\}_2Ir^{III}]^{3+}[(C_6H_5)_4B]_3{}^{3-}$		37
$[\{(CH_3)_6C_6\}_2Ir^{II}]^{2+}[PtCl_4]^{2-}$		37
$\{Arene_1\}\{Arene_2\}M^n$ $(n = I, II)$		
$\{C_6H_6\}\{(C_6H_5)_2\}Cr^{II}$	165–166	80, 87, 150
$[\{C_6H_6\}\{(C_6H_5)_2\}Cr^I]^+[HgI_3]^-$		89
$[\{C_6H_6\}\{(C_6H_5)_2\}Cr^I]^+[Cr^{II}Cl_3]^-$		85
$[\{C_6H_6\}\{(C_6H_5)_2\}Cr^I]^+[Cr^{III}(SCN)_4(NH_3)_2]^-$	150–160	81
$[\{C_6H_6\}\{(C_6H_5)_2\}Cr^I]^+[Co(CO)_4]^-$	61d	86
$[\{C_6H_6\}\{(C_6H_5)_2\}Cr^I]^+[(C_6H_5)_4B]^-$		147
$[\{C_6H_5D\}\{(C_6H_5)_2\}Cr^I]^+[(C_6H_5)_4B]^-$		147
$[\{C_6H_6\}\{(C_6H_5)_2\}Cr^I]^+[o\text{-}NH_2C_6H_6COO]^-$		87
$[\{C_6H_6\}\{(C_6H_5)_2\}Cr^I]_2{}^{2+}[C_6Cl_4O_2]^{2-}$ tetrachlorohydroquinolate		87
$[\{C_6H_5COOH\}\{(C_6H_5)_2\}Cr^I]^+[(C_6H_5)_4B]^-$	144–147	14
$[\{C_6H_5COOCH_3\}\{(C_6H_5)_2\}Cr^I]^+[(C_6H_5)_4B]^-$	183–186	14
$[\{C_6H_5CH_3\}\{o\text{-}(C_6H_5CH_2)C_6H_4CH_3\}Cr^I]^+[(C_6H_5)_4B]^-$	189–190	71
$[\{(C_6H_5)_2\}\{(p\text{-}ClC_6H_4C_6H_5\}Cr^I]^+[(C_6H_5)_4B]^-$		88
$\left.\begin{array}{l}\{C_6H_6\}\{C_5H_5\}Fe^0 \\ \{C_5H_5\}\{C_6H_7\}Fe^0\end{array}\right\}$?		73, 99
$\{Arene\}\{L\}M^n$ $(n = I, II)$		
$\{\{C_6H_6\}Ti^{II}Cl_2[AlCl_3]_2$		23, 109, 112
$[\{C_6H_6\}\{C_5H_5\}Cr^I]$	227–229	45

REFERENCES

1. ABEL, E. W., A. SINGH, and G. WILKINSON, J. Chem. Soc., **1959**, 3097.
2. BARINSKII, R. L., J. Struct. Chem. USSR, 1, 200 (1960); ibid., 3, 442 (1962).
3. BASI, J. S., and D. C. BRADLEY, Proc. Chem. Soc., **1963**, 305.
4. BAUMGÄRTNER, F., E. O. FISCHER, and U. ZAHN, Naturwissenschaften, 48, 478 (1961).
5. BAUMGÄRTNER, F., E. O. FISCHER, and U. ZAHN, Chem. Ber., 94, 2198 (1961).
6. BAUMGÄRTNER, F., and U. ZAHN, Z. Elektrochem., 64, 1046 (1960).
7. BENNETT, G. M., and E. E. TURNER, J. Chem. Soc., 105, 1057 (1914).
8. BERRY, R. S., J. Chem. Phys., 35, 29 (1961).
9. BERRY, R. S., J. Chem. Phys., 35, 2025 (1961).
10. BÖKE, K., Z. Physik. Chem. (Frankfurt), 10, 45 (1957); ibid. 11, 326 (1957).
11. BOER, D. H. W. DEN, P. C. DEN BOER, and H. C. LONGUET-HIGGINS, Mol. Phys., 5, 387 (1962).

12. BROWN, D. A., *J. Inorg. Nucl. Chem.*, **10**, 39, 49 (1959).

13. BROWN, D. A., *J. Chem. Soc.*, **1963**, 4389.

14. BURGER, T. F., and H. ZEISS, *Chem. Ind.* (London), **1962**, 183.

15. BUSH, R. W., and H. R. SNYDER, *J. Org. Chem.*, **25**, 1240 (1960).

16. CALDERAZZO, F., *Inorg. Chem.*, **3**, 810 (1964).

16a. CHATT, J., and J. M. ROBINSON, *J. Chem. Soc.*, **1965**, 843.

17. CHURCHILL, M. R., and R. MASON, *Proc. Chem. Soc.*, **1963**, 365.

18. COFFIELD, T. H., and R. D. CLOSSON, *Abstracts*, 134th Meeting Am. Chem. Soc., 1958, 58P.

19. COFFIELD, T. H., V. SANDEL, and R. D. CLOSSON, *J. Am. Chem. Soc.*, **79**, 5826 (1957).

20. CORDES, J. F., and S. SCHREINER, *Z. Anorg. Allgem. Chem.*, **299**, 87 (1959).

21. COTTON, F. A., W. A. DOLLASE, and J. S. WOOD, *J. Am. Chem. Soc.*, **85**, 1543 (1963).

22. DALY, J. J., and W. A. KORNICKER, unpublished results, Monsanto Research S.A., Zürich, Switzerland.

23. DEVRIES, H., *Rec. Trav. Chim.*, **81**, 359 (1962).

24. DICKSON, R. S., and G. WILKINSON, *Chem. Ind.* (London), **1963**, 1432.

25. DYATKINA, M. E., *Izv. Akad. Nauk SSSR. Otd. Khim. Nauk*, **1959**, 1025 (*C.A.*, **54**, 8269d): *Usp. Khim.*, **27**, 57 (1963) (*C.A.*, **52**, 14579); *Zh. Neorgan. Khim.*, **4**, 402 (1959) with E. M. SHUSTOROVICH (*C.A.*, **53**, 17666c).

26. ELSCHNER, B., and S. HERZOG, *Z. Naturforsch.*, **129**, 860 (1957).

27. FELTHAM, R. D., *J. Inorg. Nucl. Chem.*, **16**, 197 (1961).

28. FELTHAM, R. D., P. SOGO, and M. CALVIN, *J. Chem. Phys.*, **26**, 1354 (1957).

29. FISCHER, A. K., F. A. COTTON, and G. WILKINSON, *J. Phys. Chem.*, **63**, 154 (1959).

30. FISCHER, E. O., and R. BÖTTCHER, *Chem. Ber.*, **89**, 2397 (1956).

31. FISCHER, E. O., and R. BÖTTCHER, *Z. Anorg. Allgem. Chem.*, **291**, 305 (1957).

32. FISCHER, E. O., and S. BREITSCHAFT, *Angew. Chem., Intern. Ed. Engl.*, **2**, 44 (1963).

33. FISCHER, E. O., and H. BRUNNER, *Z. Naturforsch.*, **16b**, 406 (1961).

34. FISCHER, E. O., and H. BRUNNER, *Chem. Ber.*, **95**, 1999 (1962).

35. FISCHER, E. O., and H. BRUNNER, *Chem. Ber.*, **98**, 175 (1965).

36. FISCHER, E. O., and R. D. FISCHER, *Z. Naturforsch.*, **16b**, 556 (1961).

37. FISCHER, E. O., and H. P. FRITZ, *Angew. Chem.*, **73**, 353 (1961).

38. FISCHER, E. O., H. P. FRITZ, J. MANCHOT, E. PRIEBE, and R. SCHNEIDER, *Chem. Ber.*, **96**, 1418 (1963).

39. FISCHER, E. O., and W. HAFNER, *Z. Naturforsch.*, **10b**, 665 (1955).

40. FISCHER, E. O., and W. HAFNER, *Z. Anorg. Allgem. Chem.*, **286** 146 (1956).

41. FISCHER, E. O., G. JOOS, and W. MEER, *Z. Naturforsch.*, **13b**, 456 (1958).

42. FISCHER, E. O., G. JOOS, and E. VOGG, *Z. Physik. Chem.* (Frankfurt), **18**, 80 (1958).

43. FISCHER, E. O., and H. P. KÖGLER, *Angew. Chem.*, **68**, 426 (1956).

44. FISCHER, E. O., and H. P. KÖGLER, *Chem. Ber.*, **90**, 250 (1957).

45. FISCHER, E. O., and H. P. KÖGLER, *Z. Naturforsch.*, **13b**, 197 (1958).

46. FISCHER, E. O., and F. J. KOHL, *Z. Naturforsch.*, **18b**, 504 (1963).

47. FISCHER, E. O., and F. J. KOHL, *Angew. Chem.*, **76**, 98 (1964).

48. FISCHER, E. O., and H. H. LINDNER, *J. Organometal. Chem.*, **1**, 307 (1964).

49. FISCHER, E. O., and H. H. LINDNER, *J. Organometal. Chem.*, **2**, 222 (1964).

50. FISCHER, E. O., and J. MÜLLER, *Z. Naturforsch.*, **17b**, 776 (1962).

51.   FISCHER, E. O. and J. MÜLLER, *Chem. Ber.*, **96**, 3217 (1963).

52.   FISCHER, E. O., J. MÜLLER, and P. KUZEL, *Rev. Chim., Acad. Rep. Populaire Roumaine*, **7**, 827 (1962).

53.   FISCHER, E. O., and U. PIESBERGER, *Z. Naturforsch.*, **11b**, 758 (1956).

54.   FISCHER, E. O., and A. RECKZIEGEL, *Chem. Ber.*, **94**, 2204 (1961).

55.   FISCHER, E. O., and F. RÖHRSCHEID, *Z. Naturforsch.*, **17b**, 483 (1962).

56.   FISCHER, E. O., F. SCHERER, and H. O. STAHL, *Chem. Ber.*, **93**, 2065 (1960).

57.   FISCHER, E. O., and S. SCHREINER, *Chem. Ber.*, **91**, 2213 (1958).

58.   FISCHER, E. O., and S. SCHREINER, *Chem. Ber.*, **92**, 938 (1959).

59.   FISCHER, E. O., S. SCHREINER, and A. RECKZIEGEL, *Chem. Ber.*, **94**, 258 (1961).

60.   FISCHER, E. O., and J. SEEHOLZER, *Z. Anorg. Allgem. Chem.*, **312**, 244 (1961).

61a. FISCHER, E. O., and D. SEUS, *Chem. Ber.*, **89**, 1809 (1956).

61b. FISCHER, E. O., and H. O. STAHL, *Chem. Ber.*, **89**, 1805 (1956).

62.   FISCHER, E. O., and A. WIRZMÜLLER, *Chem. Ber.*, **90**, 1725 (1957).

63.   FISCHER, R. D., *Theoret. Chim. Acta*, **1**, 418 (1963).

64.   FRITZ, H. P., in F. G. A. STONE and R. WEST (eds.), *Advances in Organometallic Chemistry*, vol. 1. Academic Press, New York, 1964, p. 239.

65.   FRITZ, H. P., and W. LÜTTKE, *Fifth Intern. Conf. Coord. Chem.*, London, 1959, Chem. Soc. Spec. Publ. No. 13, 123 (1959).

66.   FRITZ, H. P., W. LÜTTKE, H. STAMMREICH, and R. FORNERIS, *Spectrochim. Acta*, **17**, 1068 (1961).

67.   FRITZ, H. P., W. LÜTTKE, H. STAMMREICH, and R. FORNERIS, *Chem. Ber.*, **92**, 3246 (1959): also S. KIRSCHNER (ed.), *Advances in the Chemistry of the Coordination Compounds*, The Macmillan Co., New York, 1961, p. 239.

68.   FURLANI, C., and E. O. FISCHER, *Z. Elektrochem.*, **61**, 481 (1957).

69.   FURLANI, C., and G. SARTORI, *Ric. Sci. Riv.*, **28**, 973 (1958) (*C.A.*, **52**, 19606).

70.   GILSON, D. F. R., and C. A. McDOWELL, *J. Chem. Phys.*, **40**, 2413 (1964).

71.   GLOCKLING, F., R. P. A. SNEEDEN, and H. ZEISS, *J. Organometal. Chem.*, **2**, 109 (1964).

72.   GLUESENKAMP, E. W., W. R. RICHARD, and J. F. K. WILSHIRE (to Monsanto Co.), U.S. Patent 3, 149,080 (Sept. 15, 1964).

73.   GREEN, M. L. H., L. PRATT, and G. WILKINSON, *J. Chem. Soc.*, **1960**, 989.

73a. HAALAND, A., *Acta Chem. Scand.*, **19**, 41 (1965).

74.   HÄHLE, J., and G. STOLZE, *Z. Naturforsch.*, **19b**, 1081 (1964).

75.   HAGIHARA, N., and H. YAMAZAKI, *J. Am. Chem. Soc.*, **81**, 3160 (1959).

76.   HAUSSER, K. H., *Naturwissenschaften*, **48**, 666 (1961).

77.   HAUSSER, K. H., *Z. Elektrochem.*, **65**, 636 (1961).

78.   HAUSSER, K. H., *Naturwissenschaften*, **48**, 426 (1961): *Z. Naturforsch.*, **14a**, 1190 (1961): *ibid.*, **16a**, 1190 (1961).

79.   HEIN, F., *Chem. Ber.*, **52**, 195 (1919): *ibid.*, **54**, 1905, 2708, 2727 (1921).

80.   HEIN, F., and K. EISFELD, *Z. Anorg. Allgem. Chem.*, **292**, 162 (1957).

81.   HEIN, F., and K. W. FISCHER, *Z. Anorg. Allgem. Chem.*, **288**, 279 (1956).

82.   HEIN, F., and K. KARTTE, *Z. Anorg. Allgem. Chem.*, **307**, 22 (1960).

83.   HEIN, F., and K. KARTTE, *Z. Anorg. Allgem. Chem.*, **307**, 52 (1960).

84.   HEIN, F., and K. KARTTE, *Z. Anorg. Allgem. Chem.*, **307**, 89 (1960).

85.   HEIN, F., and K. KARTTE, *Monatsber. Deut. Akad. Wiss.*, Berlin, **2**, 185 (1960).

86.   HEIN, F., P. KLEINERT, and W. JEHN, *Naturwissenschaften*, **44**, 34 (1956).

87.   HEIN, F., P. KLEINERT, and E. KURRAS, *Z. Anorg. Allgem. Chem.*, **289**, 229 (1957).

88. HEIN, F., and K. KLEINWÄCHTER, *Monatsber. Deut. Akad. Wiss.*, Berlin, **2**, 610 (1960).

89. HEIN, F., and E. KURRAS, *Z. Anorg. Allgem. Chem.*, **290**, 179 (1957).

90. HEIN, F., and H. REINERT, *Chem. Ber.*, **93**, 2089 (1960).

91. HEIN, F., and H. SCHEEL, *Z. Anorg. Allgem. Chem.*, **312**, 264 (1961).

92. HERWIG, W., W. METLESICS, and H. ZEISS, *J. Am. Chem. Soc.*, **81**, 6203 (1959).

93. HERWIG, W., and H. ZEISS, *J. Am. Chem. Soc.*, **79**, 6561 (1957).

94. HERWIG, W., and H. ZEISS, *J. Org. Chem.*, **23**, 1404 (1958).

95. HERWIG, W., and H. ZEISS, *J. Am. Chem. Soc.*, **81** 4798 (1959).

96. HSIUNG, H., and G. H. BROWN, *J. Electrochem. Soc.*, **110**, 1085 (1963).

97. IBERS, J. A., *J. Chem. Phys.*, **40**, 3129 (1964).

98. JONES, D., L. PRATT, and G. WILKINSON, *J. Chem. Soc.*, **1962**, 4458.

99. JONES, D., and G. WILKINSON, *Chem. Ind.* (London), **1961**, 1408.

100. KORSHUNOV, I. A., L. N. VERTYULINA, and G. A. DOMRACHEV, *J. Gen. Chem. USSR*, **32**, 9 (1962).

101. KORSHUNOV, I. A., L. N. VERTYULINA, G. A. RAZUVAEV, Y. A. SOROKIN, and G. A. DOMRACHEV, *Proc. Acad. Sci. USSR*, **122**, 769 (1958).

102. KORSHUNOV, I. A., L. N. VERTYULINA, G. A. RAZUVAEV, Y. A. SOROKIN, and G. A. DOMRACHEV, *Proc. Acad. Sci. USSR*, **122**, 1029 (1958).

103. KRAUSS, H. L., and U. DEFFNER, *Z. Naturforsch.*, **19b**, 1 (1964).

104. KRÜERKE, U., C. HOOGZAND, and W. HÜBEL, *Chem. Ber.*, **94**, 2817 (1961).

105. KURRAS, E., *Angew. Chem.*, **72**, 635 (1960).

106. LEVY, D. A., and L. E. ORGEL, *Mol. Phys.*, **4**, 93 (1961).

107. LIEHR, A. D., and C. J. BALLHAUSEN, *Acta Chem. Scand.*, **11**, 207 (1957).

108. LINNETT, J. W., *Trans. Faraday Soc.*, **52**, 904 (1956).

109. MARTIN, H., and F. VOHWINKEL, *Chem. Ber.*, **94**, 2416 (1961).

110. MILLS, O. S., and G. ROBINSON, *Proc. Chem. Soc.*, **1964**, 187.

111. MULAY, L. N., E. G. ROCHOW, and E. O. FISCHER, *J. Inorg. Nucl. Chem.*, **4**, 231 (1957).

112. NATTA, G., G. MAZZANTI, and G. PREGAGLIA, *Gazz. Chim. Ital.*, **89**, 2065 (1959), *Tetrahedron*, **8**, 86 (1960).

113. NESMEYANOV, A. N., N. A. VOL'KENAU, and I. N. BOLESOVA, *Tetrahedron Letters*, **1963**, 1725.

114. PALM, C., E. O. FISCHER, and F. BAUMGÄRTNER, *Tetrahedron Letters*, **6**, 253 (1962).

115. PARTS, L., R. L. PRUETT, and W. R. MYERS, U.S. Patent 3,101,360.

116. RAZUVAEV, G. A., and G. A. DOMRACHEV, *Tetrahedron*, **19**, 341 (1963).

117. RAZUVAEV, G. A., Y. A. SOROKIN, and G. A. DOMRACHEV, *Proc. Acad. Sci. USSR*, **111**, 1264 (1956).

118. RAZUVAEV, G. A., Y. A. SOROKIN, S. S. PETUKHOV, S. S. TSVETKOV, and Y. N. MOLIN, *Proc. Acad. Sci. USSR*, **113**, 1239 (1957).

119. ROBERTSON, R. E., and H. M. McCONNELL, *J. Phys. Chem.*, **64**, 70 (1960).

120. RUCH, E., *Z. Physik. Chem.* (Frankfurt), **6**, 356 (1956), *Z. Elektrochem.*, **61**, 913 (1957).

121. SCHRÖDER, H. P., and A. A. VLČEK, *Z. Anorg. Allgem. Chem.*, **334**, 205 (1964).

122. SHUSTOROVICH, K. M., and M. E. DYATKINA, *Russ. J. Inorg. Chem.*, **6**, 249 (1961); see also *Dokl. Akad. Nauk SSSR*, **133**, 141 (1960) (*C.A.*, **55**, 1947b): *Zh. Strukt. Khim.*, **2**, 49 (1961) (*C.A.*, **55**, 21783b): and *Dokl Akad. Nauk SSSR*, **128**, 1234 (1959) (*C.A.*, **55**, 24218e).

123. SHUSTOROVICH, K. M., and M. E. DYATKINA, *Zh. Neorgan. Khim.*, **6**, 493 (1961) (*C.A.*, **56**, 5532f): *Zh. Strukt. Khim.*, **3**, 345 (1962) (*C.A.*, **58**, 7386f).

123a. SNEEDEN, R. P. A., F. GLOCKLING, and H. ZEISS, *J. Organometal. Chem.*, in press (1966).

124. SNYDER, R. G., *Spectrochim. Acta*, **15**, 807 (1957).

125. STERNBERG, H. W., and I. WENDER, *Chem. Soc. Spec. Publ.* No. 13, 35 (1959).

126. TSUTSUI, M., and H. N. LEVY, *Proc. Chem. Soc.*, **1963**, 117.

127. TSUTSUI, M., and H. ZEISS, *Naturwissenschaften*, **44**, 420 (1957).

128. TSUTSUI, M., and H. ZEISS, *J. Am. Chem. Soc.*, **81**, 6090 (1959).

129. TSUTSUI, M., and H. ZEISS, *J. Am. Chem. Soc.*, **82**, 6255 (1960).

130. TSUTSUI, M., and H. ZEISS, *J. Am. Chem. Soc.*, **83**, 825 (1961).

131. TSVETKOV, Y. D., V. V. VOYEVODSKII, G. A. RAZUVAEV, Y. A. SOROKIN, and G. A. DOMRACHEV, *Dokl. Akad. Nauk SSSR*, **115**, 118 (1957) (*C.A.*, **52**, 2529f and **54**, 17061d).

132. TURNER, R. W., and E. L. AMMA, *J. Am. Chem. Soc.*, **85**, 4046 (1963).

133. VAINSHTEIN, E. E., and Y. F. KOPLOV, *J. Struct. Chem. USSR*, **3**, 433 (1962): *Proc. Acad. Sci. USSR*, **137**, 1117 (1961).

134. VERTYULINA, L. N., G. A. DOMRACHEV, I. A. KORSHUNOV, and G. A. RAZUVAEV, *J. Gen. Chem. USSR*, **33**, 285 (1963).

135. VLČEK, A. A., *Z. Anorg. Allgem. Chem.*, **304**, 109 (1960).

136. VLČEK, A. A., *Eighth Intern. Conf. Coord. Chem.*, 1964, Plenary Lecture.

137. VÖLTER, J., *J. Catalysis*, **3**, 297 (1964).

138. WEISS, E., *Z. Anorg. Allgem. Chem.*, **287**, 236 (1956).

139. WEISS, E., and E. O. FISCHER, *Z. Anorg. Allgem. Chem.*, **286**, 142 (1956).

140. WILKE, G., and M. KRÖNER, *Angew. Chem.*, **71**, 574 (1959).

141. YAMADA, S., H. NAKAMURA, and R. TSUCHIDA, *Bull. Chem. Soc. Japan*, **30**, 647 (1957).

142. YAMADA, S., R. TSUCHIDA, and H. YAMAZAKI, *Seventeenth Conf. Pure Appl. Chem.*, 1959, A157.

143. YAMADA, S., H. YAMAZAKI, H. NISHIKAWA, and R. TSUCHIDA, *Bull. Chem. Soc. Japan*, **33**, 481 (1960).

144. YAMAZAKI, H., M. YAMAGUCHI, and N. HAGIHARA, *Mem. Inst. Sci. Ind. Res. Osaka Univ.*, **20**, 107 (1963) (*C.A.*, **60**, 13320b), see also *Nippon Kagaku Zasshi*, **81**, 819 (1960) (*C.A.*, **56**, 1588i).

145. ZEISS, H. Chapter 8, "Organometallic Chemistry," Am. Chem. Soc. Monograph No. 147, Reinhold Publishing Corp., New York. 1960.

146. ZEISS, H., and W. HERWIG, *J. Am. Chem. Soc.*, **78**, 5959 (1956).

147. ZEISS, H., and W. HERWIG, *Ann. Chem.*, **606**, 209 (1957).

148. ZEISS, H., and W. HERWIG, *J. Am. Chem. Soc.*, **80**, 2913 (1958).

149. ZEISS, H. H., and M. TSUTSUI, *Abstracts, 126th Meeting Am. Chem. Soc.*, 1954, 29-O.

150. ZEISS, H. H., and M. TSUTSUI, *J. Am. Chem. Soc.*, **79**, 3062 (1957).

151. Unpublished results.

3

Arene-Carbonyl-Metal Complexes

INTRODUCTION

Once the chemistry of π-bis-arene-metal complexes had won general acceptance, the road was paved toward the discovery of arene-carbonyl-metal complexes. Although the first arene-carbonyl-metal complexes were reported less than seven years ago, an extensive interest in these compounds has flourished. This is undoubtedly due to the greater variety of accessible compounds, coupled with their enhanced stability and reactivity as compared to π-bis-arene-metal complexes.

These properties gave the impetus to thorough studies of the chemistry of the complexes, both from the standpoint of the mechanism of their formation and the alteration of the chemical properties of the benzenoid compound caused by π-bonding to transition metals. Although the arene-carbonyl-metal complexes are not naturally occurring products, it now appears that much can be learned from their chemistry concerning fundamental processes involving rearrangements, hydrogen transfer, and other types of catalytic activities at metal centers.

METHODS OF PREPARATION

The preparation of bis-arene-metal complexes from transition metal halides requires reduction of the metal ion to a low valency. The availability of carbonyl-metal complexes containing metals in low valence states led to experiments designed to explore the possibility of exchanging one or more ligands from such complexes with the concurrent or subsequent formation of a π-bond to a benzenoid molecule. Consequently, it is not surprising that this method of preparation was reported almost simultaneously from a number of laboratories (34,76,79,80).

44

Carbonyl-Metal(0) and Benzenoid Compound

The exchange of three molecules of carbon monoxide from a carbonyl-metal(0) complex by a benzenoid compound has led to a large series of arene complexes, a list of which is given in Table 3–2:

$$Metal(CO)_n + Arene \rightarrow \{Arene\}Metal(CO)_{n-3} + 3\ CO$$

Although the transition metal, the arene and the reaction conditions have been varied, it has not been possible to exchange all carbonyl ligands on the same metal center by two benzenoid molecules. It thus appears as if either the arene causes a strengthening of the bond to the remaining ligands or that the removal of one molecule of carbon monoxide from the parent complex proceeds easily, allowing the approach of the arene for further displacement of carbonyl ligands. Recently, evidence has been cited (86) which suggests that it is possible initially to displace one molecule of carbon monoxide from a metal carbonyl and subsequently two more carbonyl ligands by an intramolecular process:

$$Metal(CO)_n + Arene \rightarrow \{Arene\}Metal(CO)_{n-1} + CO$$

$$\{Arene\}Metal(CO)_{n-1} \rightarrow \{Arene\}Metal(CO)_{n-3} + 2\ CO$$

Arguments have, however, been presented against this view (80).

The major advantage of using carbonyl-transition metal compounds as starting materials is the relative ease with which π-complexes of *substituted* benzenoid compounds can be prepared. Hexacarbonyl-chromium(0) has most widely been used in the preparation of arene-tricarbonyl-chromium(0) complexes, but other available carbonyl-transition metal complexes have also been utilized.

Vanadium. Vanadium(0) forms a hexacarbonyl which reacts with benzenoid molecules such as benzene, toluene, xylene, and mesitylene (7). The resulting complexes are salts in which the metal appears to have undergone disproportionation:

$$2\ V(CO)_6 + C_6H_6 \rightarrow [\{C_6H_6\}V^I(CO)_4]^+[V^{-I}(CO)_6]^- + 2\ CO$$

The ionic structure of the light-sensitive compound is supported by the non-volatility of the compound, its solubility in water and its insolubility in hydrocarbon solvents. The cation of the complex forms water-insoluble tetraphenylborate and hexafluorophosphate salts:

$$[\{C_6H_6\}V^I(CO)_4]^+[V^{-I}(CO)_6]^- + NaB(C_6H_5)_4 \rightarrow$$
$$[\{C_6H_6\}V^I(CO)_4]^+[B(C_6H_5)_4]^- + Na[V^{-I}(CO)_6]$$

Vanadium is the only representative of the Group VA transition metal family from which π-arene-carbonyl-metal complexes have been prepared. It is surprising that vanadium(I), being isoelectronic with titanium(0), forms a benzene-tetracarbonyl-vanadium(I) ion, whereas the corresponding titanium complex is not known. The only benzene-titanium complex which has been described is the complex compound, benzene-titanium(II) chloride bis-aluminum trichloride, the structure of which is not clear (21,70,78).

Chromium, Molybdenum, Tungsten. By far the greatest number of arene-carbonyl-metal complexes isolated contain chromium(0) as the central metal. The reaction of hexacarbonyl-chromium(0) with benzene or substituted benzenoid molecules, under more or less stringent conditions, have led to a multitude of compounds. These are of particular interest because of the greater reactivity of the arene ligand in these compounds as compared to the bis-arene-metal complexes. Arene-tricarbonyl-chromium(0) complexes of functionally substituted benzenoid compounds are accessible by the reaction:

$$Cr(CO)_6 + C_6H_5X \rightarrow \{C_6H_5X\}Cr(CO)_3 + 3\ CO$$

$X = $ H, F, OH, NH$_2$, COOH, CH$_2$OH, OCH$_3$, N(CH$_3$)$_2$, CH$_3$COO—, —CH$_2$COOH, —COOCH$_3$ (for references see Table 3–2)

Improved yields were obtained by working in open systems, which facilitated the removal of gaseous carbon monoxide, driving the reaction toward completion (87). Compared to vanadium, three molecules of carbon monoxide are eliminated rather than two. Since benzene-tricarbonyl-chromium(0) is diamagnetic, it is tempting to consider the six electrons from the metal as occupying pairwise three $3d$-orbitals, while the twelve electrons from the ligands (two from each carbonyl ligand and six from the π-electron system of the benzene molecule) in the classical sense fill the six d^2sp^3-hybrid orbitals. The metal complex thus attains the much discussed noble-gas configuration. In similar fashion vanadium(I) in the benzene-tetracarbonyl-vanadium(I) ion can accept two more electrons (one more carbonyl ligand) to attain the krypton configuration. Although this type of reasoning may lead only by chance to the correct prediction of magnetic properties, and despite vigorous opposition, it remains curious indeed that many more complexes of noble-gas configuration are known than complexes with fewer or more electrons than the corresponding noble-gas complement.

Several disubstituted benzene molecules have been attached to the group tricarbonyl-chromium(0). If two unlike substituents are situated *ortho* or *meta* to each other, the compound obtained should be capable of existing in enantiomeric forms, provided the metal does not shift from one side of the benzene nucleus to the other.

This type of movement within the complex does not occur, as is shown by the resolution of *m*-methoxybenzoic acid-tricarbonyl-chromium(0) (65). The racemic acid formed a pair of diastereoisomeric salts with brucine and the enantiomeric acids could be recovered after fractional crystallization of these salts. Figure 3–1 shows the enantiomeric acids, the filled circles, A, representing COOH, the open ones, B, the CH_3O— substituent.

Benzenoid compounds containing two arene nuclei not fused to each other are capable of forming bis-tricarbonyl-chromium(0) complexes. Naphthalene gives only the mono-tricarbonyl-chromium(0) complex (34)

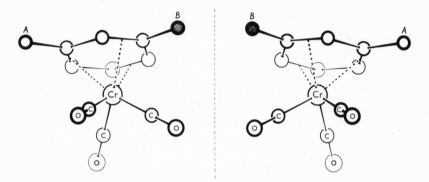

Fig. 3–1. Enantiomeric *m*-methoxybenzoic acid-tricarbonyl-chromium(0) complexes.

in contrast to biphenyl, which forms the bis-tricarbonyl-chromium(0) derivative (23). This observation may be extended to higher homologs such as anthracene (31,111), phenanthrene (31,60), chrysene (31), and pyrene (60), all of which form only *mono*-tricarbonyl-chromium(0) complexes, whereas *bis*-tricarbonyl-chromium(0) complexes of diphenylmethane, diphenylethane, *trans*-stilbene (23), and 1,4-diphenylbutadiene (5) may be obtained. The latter is particularly noteworthy since the 1,4-butadiene entity is capable of acting independently as a chelate ligand to iron (5,67):

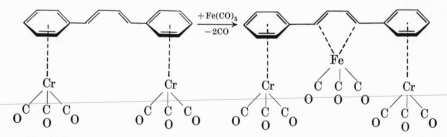

Much fruitless effort has been spent on attempts to prepare bis-arene chromium(0) complexes directly from hexacarbonyl-chromium(0). A number of *para*-cyclophane molecules were heated with hexacarbonyl-chromium(0) in an endeavor to remove all six carbonyl ligands and prepare a bis-arene-chromium(0) complex with the chromium atom sandwiched neatly between the aromatic nuclei (16).   In all cases complexes were obtained which had structures m,n-cyclophane- *mono*-[tricarbonyl-chromium(0)] or m,n-cyclophane-*bis*-[tricarbonyl-chromium(0):

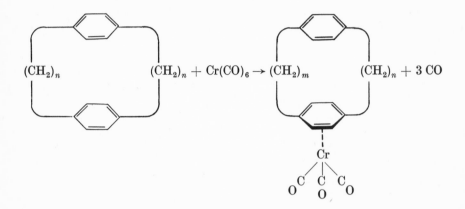

The other transition metals of the Group VIA family (Mo and W) likewise give uncharged arene-tricarbonyl complexes such as benzene-tricarbonyl-molybdenum(0) (34,88,110) and benzene-tricarbonyl-tungsten(0)(34).   There is very little difference in the stability of these complexes, although their melting points decrease as the atomic weight increases within the family.

In an attempt to establish whether biphenylene may be considered as bibenzo-cyclobutadiene, the hydrocarbon was heated in the presence of triglyme-tricarbonyl-molybdenum(0) (9).   The products isolated contained one or two tricarbonyl-molybdenum(0) groups linked to the benzenoid rings:

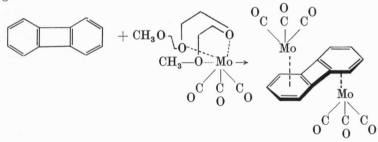

On the basis of the detection (by X-ray crystal data) of a center of symmetry in the latter compound, the *trans*-configuration was established.

Manganese. Elemental manganese (a Group VIIA element) has one more electron than chromium in its outer sphere. Hence it is not surprising that only arene-tricarbonyl-manganese(I) salts have been isolated. The cations of these salts are diamagnetic and thus isoelectronic with the arene-tricarbonyl-chromium(0) complexes. Only benzenoid *hydrocarbons* have been employed in reaction with carbonyl derivatives of manganese (12,112,113) in the presence of aluminum chloride:

$$C_6H_6 + Mn(CO)_5Cl \rightarrow \{C_6H_6\}Mn^I(CO)_3Cl + 2\ CO$$

Insoluble perchlorate, tetraphenylborate, triiodide, and reineckate salts may conveniently be precipitated and isolated (113):

$$[\{C_6H_6\}Mn^I(CO)_2]^+Cl^- + Na[B(C_6H_5)_4] \rightarrow$$
$$[\{C_6H_6\}Mn^I(CO)_3]^+[B(C_6H_5)_4]^- + NaCl$$

Iron, Cobalt. Representative Group VIII metals, which, aside from two $4s$ electrons, possess six, seven, or eight $3d$ electrons have not been intensively studied, with the exception of iron ($3d^6 4s^2$) and cobalt ($3d^7 4s^2$). The structures of arene-carbonyl-Group VIII metal complexes are complicated by multicentered arrangements involving more than one metal atom per molecule. Accordingly, carbonyl-iron complexes react with *m*- or *p*-divinylbenzene to yield mono-arene-hexacarbonyl-diiron complexes (67), while mercury(II) bis-[tetracarbonyl-cobalt(−I)] on heating with benzene in the presence of aluminum chloride yields a salt, the composition of the cation, of charge +1, being tris-benzene-dicarbonyl-tricobalt (10,26). For the latter ion the complex structure was suggested on the basis of analyses and decomposition products of the insoluble tetraphenylborate or reineckate:

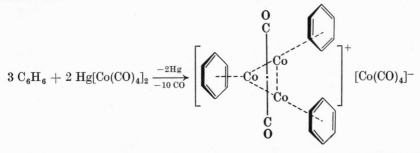

An attempt to form an arene-carbonyl-iron complex by ligand exchange between pentacarbonyl-iron(0) and bis-biphenyl-chromium(0) caused disproportionation to a bis-biphenyl-chromium(I) salt, the ions of which were separately precipitated as the respective tetraphenylborate or tetraethylammonium salts (47):

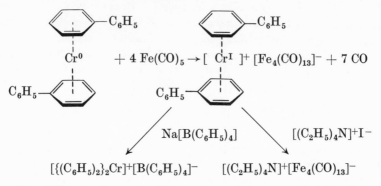

$$[\{(C_6H_5)_2\}_2Cr]^+[B(C_6H_5)_4]^- \qquad [(C_2H_5)_4N]^+[Fe_4(CO)_{13}]^-$$

The following route to the unknown benzene-tricarbonyl-iron(0) *via* the known cyclohexadienyl-complex (28) has been suggested but not realized (17):

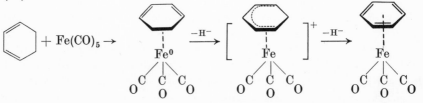

The anthracene-tricarbonyl-iron(0) and similar complexes have been isolated (46,60) and probably should be considered to possess a localized diene-bond linked to the central iron:

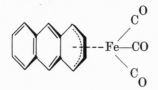

The isomerization of dihydroindene to a supposed cyclononatetraene on heating with dodecacarbonyl-triiron shows the tendency of iron to complex with olefinic molecules (59,60):

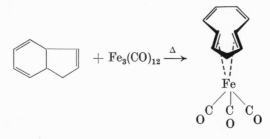

LIGAND EXCHANGES

Aside from the general method of preparation just described, a few special reactions have been shown to yield arene-carbonyl-metal complexes. The first report to appear in the literature (33) for the preparation of benzene tricarbonyl-chromium(0) describes a ligand exchange reaction between bis-benzene-chromium(0) and hexacarbonyl-chromium(0):

$$\{C_6H_6\}_2Cr^0 + Cr(CO)_6 \rightarrow 2\ \{C_6H_6\}Cr(CO)_3$$

The reaction requires vigorous conditions (sealed tube 220°) and gives mediocre yields. Attempts to produce the same product from a reaction of carbon monoxide with bis-benzene-chromium(0) failed at temperatures below 170° and produced only hexacarbonyl-chromium(0) at higher temperatures.

The production of benzene-tricarbonyl-chromium(0) by the reaction of hexacarbonyl-chromium with either benzene or bis-benzene-chromium(0) involves the exchange of three carbonyl ligands by one benzene nucleus. This observation and the exchange of one carbonyl in arene-tricarbonyl-chromium(0) complexes by another neutral ligand (96) have in recent years led to a detailed study (100,104,105) of the mechanism of carbonyl ligand exchange.

Carbonyl Exchange

The exchange of carbonyl ligands between arene-tricarbonyl-chromium(0) and carbon monoxide containing radioactive carbon takes place under the influence of ultraviolet irradiation (100):

$$(^{14}CO)_{sol'n} + \{C_6H_6\}Cr(CO)_3 \xrightarrow{h\nu} (CO)_{sol'n} + \{C_6H_6\}Cr(CO)_2(^{14}CO)$$

Comparative studies on the rate of carbonyl exchange between radioactive carbon monoxide and the various arene-carbonyl-complexes of the three Groups VIA metals, Cr, Mo, and W, showed a marked decrease in rate of exchange with increasing atomic weight of the central atom. It was found that under comparative conditions (intensity of light, concentration, solvent, and time of irradiation) toluene-tricarbonyl-chromium(0), -molybdenum(0), and -tungsten(0) underwent exchange to the extent of 78%, 20%, and 0%, respectively. It is not entirely clear, however, whether this is a kinetic or a thermodynamic effect, or a combination of both.

Arene Exchange

The exchange of one benzenoid compound for another has been used for the preparation of a few tricarbonyl-arene-metal(0) complexes (68,76) as exemplified by the synthesis of dimethylaniline-tricarbonyl-chromium(0) (55):

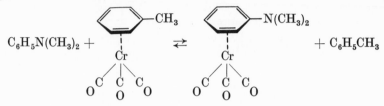

$$C_6H_5N(CH_3)_2 +$$

$$\rightleftarrows$$

$$+ C_6H_5CH_3$$

This type of reaction is an equilibrium process and is favored by the usual concentration effects or by the removal of the ligand displaced from the starting material.

A discussion of the possible mechanism of the formation of arene-tricarbonyl-chromium(0) is perhaps best preceded by consideration of the mechanism of the exchange of one benzenoid compound for another in preformed arene-tricarbonyl-metal(0) complexes:

$$\text{Arene}_1 + \{\text{Arene}_2\}Cr(CO)_3 \rightleftharpoons \text{Arene}_2 + \{\text{Arene}_1\}Cr(CO)_3$$

This reaction has been studied in detail from a kinetic standpoint by the powerful techniques of radiochemistry. Thus a series of ^{14}C-tagged benzenoid compounds of the general formula, $\{*\text{arene}\}M(CO)_3$, have been prepared by ligand exchange in a thermal process (101,102,103,104,105):

$$\{\text{Arene}\}M(CO)_3 + *\text{Arene} \rightleftharpoons \{*\text{Arene}\}M(CO)_3 + \text{Arene}$$

The effects of the metal (104), the substituent in the benzenoid compound (101,104), and the solvent (105) on the rate of reaction have been studied with the purpose of elucidating the mechanism of ligand-exchange reactions.

Mechanism of Exchanges

As a model for the study of the ligand exchange the system ^{14}C-tagged benzene/untagged benzene-tricarbonyl-chromium(0) was chosen:

$$*C_6H_6 + \{C_6H_6\}Cr(CO)_3 \rightleftharpoons \{*C_6H_6\}Cr(CO)_3 + C_6H_6$$

The rate of exchange was studied by isolating the mixture of tagged and untagged benzene-tricarbonyl-chromium(0) and measuring its activity. The rate of reaction was measured by the change in activity of the complexes isolated from aliquots removed at various time intervals. A series of observed reaction rates were then calculated from a first order integrated rate expression (102). The dependence of this rate on starting concentrations (relative concentration varied by factors of 10–20) and temperature (140°, 160, and 180°) led to the conclusion that the reaction is second-order in the complex and *ca.* $\frac{1}{3}$-order in benzene. The dependence of the calculated rate on the initial concentration can be reconciled by the consideration that two mechanisms for the exchange are operating. Thus, if one rate-determining step (A) is assumed to be second-order in the complex and another much slower step (B) is assumed to be first-order in the complex and first-order in benzene, the data can be well accommodated. From the temperature dependency the activation parameters were calculated for both mechanisms. The rate-determining steps may be depicted thus:

A

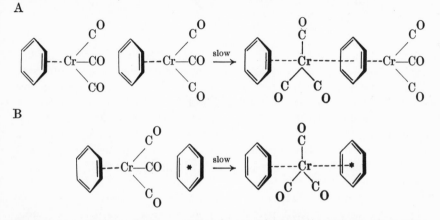

B

Since A in contrast to B does not involve any increase in activity, the author further assumes that the slow, rate-determining step to the formation of the dimeric activated complex is followed by two fast steps: C, the "Walden inversion" of one of the tricarbonyl-chromium groups, causes the liberation of one molecule of benzene and a very active intermediate $Cr(CO)_3$; the latter in a distinct and fast step (D) then undergoes reaction with a second molecule of benzene:

C

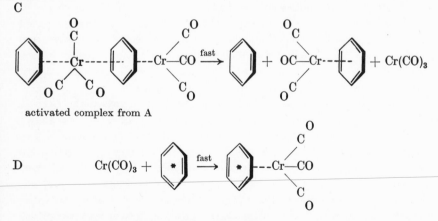

activated complex from A

The sequence of steps A → C → D accounts for the rate-determining step, which is second-order in the complex, while the sequence B → E is envisioned as a direct exchange of a tagged benzene molecule for an untagged one by a fast step (E):

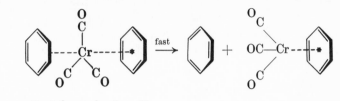

activated complex from B

The activation parameters for both mechanisms show that the enthalpy of activation of step B is lower than for step A. The fact that sequence $A \rightarrow C \rightarrow D$ is still favored over $B \rightarrow E$ is borne out by the large difference in entropies of activation, $A: \Delta S^{\ddagger} = -4.2$, $B: \Delta S^{\ddagger} = 20.5$. It is not unreasonable that the probability for changing rotational to vibrational degrees of freedom is larger in the formation of the activated complex by A than by B, since the benzene molecule to which the new bond is formed is already locked in a planar position prior to the formation of the activated complex *via* route A. This is not the case in B. A rationale based on the collision frequency, a steric parameter, and the observed frequency factors of the Arrhenius equation led to the conclusion that mechanism A was favored because of the larger "reaction radius" (collision diameter) of the reactants involved in this step as compared to those involved in step B (102).

The influence of the solvent showed that there was no change in mechanism by changing the dielectric constant of the medium. There was, however, an increase in reaction rate with increasing dielectric constant (105). By using standard procedures the dipole moments of the activated complexes formed by A and B were calculated to be of the order of 25 and 15 Debye units, respectively. This is in reasonable agreement with that expected for the two complexes, since the former would be expected to show a larger polarizability. The fact that the dipole moments of the activated complexes are much larger than those of the reactants and products is likewise in agreement with that expected for the proposed mechanisms.

An increase in dielectric constant of the solvent increased the over-all rate of exchange of the benzenoid ligand. In a detailed study it was shown that this effect could be traced to an increase in the rate-determining step A and in particular that such drastic lowering of the energy of activation outweighed the decrease in the Arrhenius frequency factor. By contrast, the frequency factor for formation of the activated complex by step B was found to be independent of the solvent, while the energy of activation is changed only slightly. This effect agrees with the influence of solvent on the dipole moment of arene-tricarbonyl-chromium(0), indicating that it is the π-bonded benzene nucleus of the complex which is capable of functioning as acceptor for donor-type solvents. In solvents of higher dielectric constant, solvation of the benzene nucleus should hinder approach to the back side of the tricarbonyl chromium group in step A and thus decrease the steric factor in accordance with observation (104). Solvation should have no effect on B (the approach of a benzene molecule to benzene-tricarbonyl-chromium) if this were to take place from the tricarbonyl side of the complex. The dependency of rate constants on dielectric constant of the solvent was hence interpreted to be a further piece of evidence for the mechanistic path postulated.

The rate of exchange of substituted benzene-tricarbonyl-metal(0) complexes with the corresponding radioactive arenes was studied, to determine the influence of the central metal and the substituents on the process:

$$\{C_6H_5X\}M(CO)_3 + {}^*C_6H_5X \rightarrow \{{}^*C_6H_5X\}M(CO)_3 + C_6H_5X$$

$$M = Cr, Mo, W$$

$$X = H, CH_3, Cl$$

Again no change in mechanism from that observed for the model compound was found. In all cases the mechanism leading to a dimeric arene-tricarbonyl metal(0) complex (A) is favored by a factor of 10 over that leading to the activated complex "bis-benzene-tricarbonyl-metal" (B). This is interpreted as evidence for the enhanced tendency of the benzenoid compound to act as an acceptor when it is coordinated to a transition metal (105).

The rate of exchange obtained from experiments performed under comparable conditions on various toluene-tricarbonyl-metal(0) complexes (104) supports the general mechanism and shows that the rate constants for both mechanisms are larger for toluene-tricarbonyl-molybdenum(0) by a factor of ca. 100 than for the tungsten(0) complex. On the other hand, the rate constant for the tungsten(0) complex is ca. 100 times larger than that for toluene-tricarbonyl-chromium(0).

This order is reflected in a decrease in activation energies for both A and B in proceeding along the series: Cr, W, Mo as the central atom, a decrease which is not compensated by the decrease in steric factor for the same series. No satisfactory explanation for this curious observation has been given.

A chlorine substituent in the benzenoid compound enhances the rate of exchange relative to the benzene complex, while a methyl substituent retards it. Apparently, the electron-releasing substituent disfavors the formation of both the activated complexes (by route A or B), while the electron-withdrawing substituent favors their formation. This makes the reaction appear as an electrophilic attack by the complexed benzenoid compound on the metal or, conversely, as nucleophilic attack by the central metal of one molecule on the aromatic portion of another complex. Both these possibilities appear rather unusual, and the conclusions should be considered as tentative since one of the substituted arenes chosen is capable of reacting *via* a mesomeric intermediate; the other is not.

A negative *rho*-constant is implied, but the three points do not allow a reasonable evaluation of its magnitude. Since the development of charge in proceeding to the activated complex may be neglected, the explanation for a negative *rho* may be sought in the decreased stability of complex containing a lower electron density in the benzenoid ring compared to one having a higher electron density.

Comparative studies of photochemically induced exchange of benzenoid compounds should perhaps reflect this effect:

$$Ar^*X + \{ArX\}Cr(CO)_3 \xrightarrow{h\nu} \{Ar^*X\}Cr(CO)_3 + ArX$$

However, the order of exchange observed $(X = H > Cl > CH_3)$ in the reaction did not parallel the order found for the thermal exchange $(Cl > H > CH_3)$. This may be an effect caused by the change in chromophore rather than a reflection of stability or ease of formation of the activated complexes.

Mechanism of Formation of Arene-Carbonyl-Metal Complexes

Attempts have been made to apply the experience and knowledge acquired from the arene exchange reactions to the elucidation of the mechanism of the formation of arene-tricarbonyl-metal(0) compounds (92). Preliminary efforts showed that *p*-xylene-tricarbonyl-molybdenum(0) could be formed in good yield from hexacarbonyl-molybdenum(0) and *p*-xylene (88):

$$Mo(CO)_6 + 1,4\text{-}(CH_3)_2C_6H_4 \rightarrow 3\ CO + \{1,4\text{-}(CH_3)_2C_6H_4\}Mo(CO)_3$$

Apparent orders of 0.5 and 0.3 for the consumption of hexacarbonyl-molybdenum and *p*-xylene, respectively, were found to agree with the rate of carbon monoxide liberated (92). This unsatisfactory result did not allow any conclusions to be drawn concerning the mechanism of formation of arene-tricarbonyl-metal(0) complexes. The preparation has been regarded as a new type of electrophilic attack on the benzenoid compound (80), since the influence of substituents is roughly parallel to that of other electrophilic aromatic substitution reactions. Electron-releasing substituents such as $(CH_3)_2N$, CH_3, etc. $(\sigma < 0)$ facilitate the reaction, whereas electron-withdrawing groups such as the halogens, $COOCH_3$ $(\sigma > 0)$, retard it.

ARENE-CARBONYL-METAL COMPLEXES CONTAINING OTHER LIGANDS

The carbonyl-metal(0) complexes constitute a convenient source of a number of transition metals in oxidation state zero. It has been shown how a large series of complexes can be prepared by the exchange of one, two, or three carbonyl ligands for one benzenoid compound. The reluctance of the resulting arene-carbonyl-metal(0) complexes to exchange the remaining carbonyl ligands for another arene molecule has been discussed. It appears as if the tricarbonyl-chromium(0) group functions *per se* as a stable ligand acceptor for benzenoid compounds. The mechanism for the exchange of one arene for another on tricarbonyl-complexes of chromium, molybdenum, and tungsten have been well demonstrated. However, the introduction of ^{14}C-tagged carbon monoxide into arene-tricarbonyl-metal(0) under the influence of light (100) indicates that it is indeed possible to exchange at least one carbonyl for another. It has not been unambiguously proven whether such an exchange occurs by a mechanism involving removal of one carbonyl ligand prior to the introduction of another, or whether the exchange occurs *via* displacement. It may even be possible that one carbonyl ligand is first removed and an intermediate is formed which contains a solvent molecule bonded to the site which the carbonyl left; or that it is dimeric and contains a metal-metal bond.

Photolytic and Thermal Exchange

Whatever structure the proposed intermediate may have, it is capable of giving isolable complexes with a large variety of molecules that can function as donor ligands. In general, only one nucleophilic molecule may be introduced into arene-tricarbonyl complexes (32,80,91,96):

$$\{arene\}M^0(CO)_3 + L \xrightarrow{h\nu} \{arene\}M^0(CO)_2L + CO$$

L = pyridine, triphenylphosphine, nitriles, etc.

The first complex of this type reported (32) contains a molecule of an olefin as a ligand, aside from carbonyl and arene ligands. If this reaction is compared to the arene-exchange reaction previously discussed, a striking difference is noted. Of the two plausible competing mechanisms for the arene-exchange reaction, the one is favored which involves nucleophilic attack on the arene bound to a metal. In the exchange of a carbonyl for another ligand, the complex or an intermediate generated from it behaves as an electron acceptor.

The stability of the resulting compounds, $\{arene\}M(CO)_nL$ is for a given benzenoid compound dependent both on the metal and the ligand L (95,96,97). The thermodynamic stability should be distinguished from the rate with which the complex is formed. The latter kinetic effect is dependent on a number of factors which have not been studied in detail.

The reaction causing the replacement of one molecule of carbon monoxide by another ligand molecule has been described for pure carbonyl-metal compounds and also for cyclopentadienyl-tricarbonyl-metal derivatives (114).

Mechanism of Exchange

The thermodynamic evidence is discussed later, and only the general trends are considered here. Many of the conclusions drawn are based on arguments concerning back-donation to the carbonyl ligands from the metal in complexes $\{C_6H_5X\}Cr^0(CO)_2L$. It is held in general that substituents X (having positive *sigma* values) which are electron-withdrawing decrease the extent of back-donation from the metal to the carbonyl ligand by decreasing the electron density on the metal. This effect can be recognized in the increase in carbonyl frequency and a decrease in dipole moment of the complex. The reverse is the effect of an electron-donating substituent, Y:

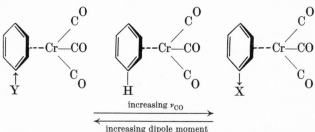

increasing ν_{CO}

increasing dipole moment

This argument was then used to interpret the effect of substituents X in the arene on the strength of the metal-L bond (L being pyridine or piperidine). It was observed that the stability of both pyridine and piperidine complexes of the type $\{arene\}Cr(CO)_2L$ decreased along the series containing arene = $\{1,4\text{-}(CH_3OOC)_2C_6H_4\}$, $\{C_6H_6\}$, $\{1,3,5\text{-}(CH_3)_3C_6H_3\}$. For the case of piperidine the argument is plausible that an electron-withdrawing substituent such as $COOCH_3$ decreases the electron density on the metal and this increases the strength of the coordinate-covalent bond. On the other hand, the methyl substituent, being an electron supplier, would increase the electron density on the metal and thus in effect decrease the tendency of the metal to accept electrons, thereby weakening the coordinate-covalent bond. However, this argument does not hold as an explanation for the same order of stability of the pyridine complexes, since in this case back-donation could indeed play a roll in contributing to the combined "bond strength."

The problem of comparing bond strengths to ligands L in complexes containing arene ligands with substituents in different positions is not a simple one. These should likewise be dependent on the influence of the symmetry of the arene ligand on both the location and availability of the orbitals necessary for acceptance on back-donation to a ligand L.

The order of stability is, however, not reversed for ligands L better capable of accepting electrons by back-donation from the metal (95,96). This is explained in terms of the contribution of the σ-bond from the ligand relative to the back-donation to the over-all strength of the L-metal bond.

The *sigma*-bond portion is weakened by electron supplying substituents on the arene while the extent of back-donation should increase. In agreement with observation it is contended that the former effect dominates the over-all bond strength. The relative bond strength, however, is determined qualitatively by criteria based on the ease of decomposition. For a more quantitative treatment of these effects on the Cr—L bond strength (97,98) see the section on Physical Properties.

REACTIONS OF ARENE-CARBONYL-METAL COMPLEXES

It was demonstrated in the previous chapter how benzenoid compounds lose their aromatic reactivity on π-bonding to transition metals, either because of the modification of the aromatic characteristics brought about by the involvement of the π-electron cloud in bonding to the metal, or because of the instability of the complexes toward either nucleophilic or electrophilic reagents. By contrast it was soon found that in mono-arene-carbonyl-metal complexes the benzenoid portion showed a very marked tendency to undergo nucleophilic substitution and, among other reactions, also electrophilic substitution. Aside from the availability of a larger array of substituted benzenoid carbonyl complexes, an explanation for this enhanced reactivity (compared to bis-benzenoid complexes) may in part be sought in the "unsymmetrical" nature of the complexes. This "unsymmetrical" nature affects the polarizability before or during reaction. Other factors such as the greater stability of the carbonyl-metal complexes and the decreased steric requirement for reactions initiated at the central metal may account for the greater variety of reactions studied.

Electrophilic Substitution

The most reasonable suggestions for π-type bonding between a benzenoid compound and a transition metal involves some degree of donation of electrons to the metal. This direction of electronic transfer would create an electron deficiency on the arene and leave it less prone to electrophilic attack than the free arene. This is borne out by the great preponderance of reactions proceeding *via* nucleophilic rather than electrophilic attack.

That such a lowering in electron density is caused by complexing to a transition metal could be shown by comparing the acid strength of benzoic acid with that of benzoic acid-tricarbonyl-chromium(0) (36,80):

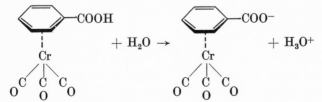

The pK_a of the π-bonded acid was 4.77 (compared to 5.68 for benzoic acid)

showing that the "electron-withdrawing" power of the tricarbonyl-chromium(0) group is similar to that of the nitro group in the *para*-position (pK_a for *p*-nitrobenzoic acid, 4.48). Conversely the pK_b of aniline is increased from 11.70 to 13.31 on π-bonding to tricarbonyl-chromium(0).

However, despite the fact that no Friedel-Crafts products of bis-arene-metal(0) complexes have been obtained, it was found possible to acetylate benzene-tricarbonyl-chromium(0) under mild conditions (24,48,84):

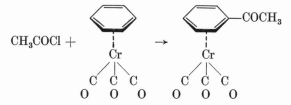

The instability of the π-bond to Lewis' acids under more severe conditions may well be the reason for failure of bis-benzene-metal(0) derivatives to undergo this reaction. It is significant to note that electron-donating substituents (whether of the $+I$ inductive or the $-I,+T$ type) do not enhance Friedel-Crafts' acylation (80).

A study dealing with the directional effect of a methyl group in the arene (48) showed that in contrast to free toluene, which gives predominantly the *p*-isomer ($p:o:m$ 92:8:0), π-bonded toluene reacted slower under the same conditions and yielded all three isomers in the relative percentages, $p:o:m$ of 46:39:15. The explanation, founded partially on the proposed C_{3v}-symmetry of benzenoid compounds when bonded to transition metal, carries less weight since recent X-ray studies disagree with this symmetry of the arene portion of the molecule (15). The differences in orientation and ease of reaction between free and π-bonded arene should perhaps be sought in the reluctance toward formation of the same transition state when the benzenoid compound is π-bonded to a metal.

In general, the arene-tricarbonyl-metal(0) complex is unstable to strong acid, and thus is inaccessible to electrophilic substitutions such as nitration and sulfonation.

The methylation of aniline-tricarbonyl-chromium(0) is significant, since the reaction apparently does not proceed beyond the monomethylated product (80), another confirmation of the decreased nucleophilicity of the aromatic system:

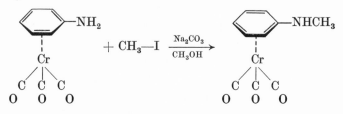

Nucleophilic Substitution

Nucleophilic attacks on benzenoid molecules are relatively rare reactions, occurring either in compounds containing strongly electron-withdrawing groups, such as the nitro groups in picryl chloride, or in compounds which are not activated in this way by the use of very powerful nucleophiles such as organometallic compounds. Such nucleophilic substitution is often accompanied by apparent rearrangements which can be explained in terms of symmetrical benzyne intermediates.

The reaction of picryl chloride with an alkoxide has been classified as a nucleophilic attack on aromatic carbon. The reaction of mono-nitro-chlorobenzene is much slower, and that of chlorobenzene has no significance as a preparative method. The facile reaction of chlorobenzene-tricarbonyl-chromium(0) with sodium methoxide to yield anisole-tricarbonyl-chromium demonstrates the enhanced reactivity of the π-bonded benzenoid nucleus toward nucleophiles (80):

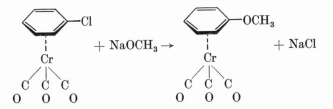

Many reactions of functional groups have been described which do not proceed by nucleophilic displacement on the aromatic carbon, but on the group attached to the π-bonded arene. Thus, saponification of alkyl-benzoate-tricarbonyl-metal(0) proceeds with ease (65,80) to the corresponding acids. This is even the preferred method of preparing tricarbonyl-metal(0) complexes of aryl-substituted acids, since the direct route gives unsatisfactory yields (34,65,76,80):

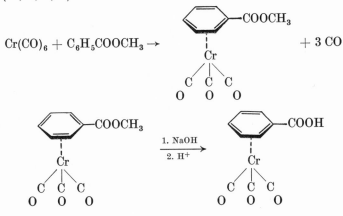

The reaction used in the pioneering work on the determination of the structures of Hein's organochromium compounds involved the removal from the metal of what was later found to be π-bonded benzenoid compounds by reduction with lithium aluminum hydride. Under mild conditions the esters of arene-tricarbonyl-chromium(0) can be reduced in good yields to the corresponding alcohols with the same reagent without decomposition of the complex (80). Thus benzyl alcohol-tricarbonyl-chromium can be prepared by two independent routes (76,80):

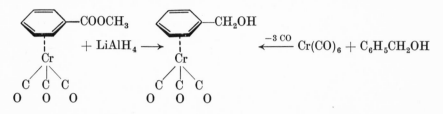

In a manner analogous to the protection of a carboxylic acid group by esterification, amino or hydroxyl groups can be protected by facile acetylation (80):

$$\{C_6H_5OH\}Cr(CO)_3 + (CH_3CO)_2O \rightarrow \{C_6H_5OCOCH_3\}Cr(CO)_3$$

$$\{C_6H_5NH_2\}Cr(CO)_3 + (CH_3CO)_2O \rightarrow \{C_6H_5NHCOCH_3\}Cr(CO)_3$$

Nucleophilic Addition

An unusual reaction of arene-tricarbonyl-manganese(I) involving the strong nucleophile, phenyllithium, has been shown to proceed with addition of the nucleophile to the arene (56). In effect, the compound isolated is the intermediate one would expect in a hypothetical nucleophilic substitution of hydrogen on aromatic carbon by phenyllithium:

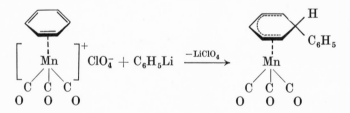

The phenyl substituent was first believed to be situated *endo* to the metal but later the *exo*-position was favored (57) because of the publication of an X-ray structure for an analogous compound (11). The product of the addition of phenyllithium has been named "phenylcyclohexadienyl-tricarbonyl-manganese(0)." Although the structure has not been unambiguously proved, physical evidence appears to support it. For the purpose of this discussion, let us consider what is meant by writing the structure as shown in the first formula. If the phenyl anion adds to the essentially uncharged benzene nucleus of the cationic complex, and there is no reduction of the metal by complete transfer of an electron to the manganese in oxidation state +I, then the benzene molecule has become a phenylcyclohexadienyl anion:

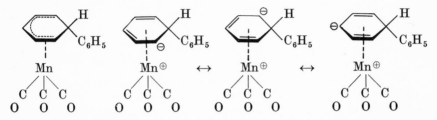

The neutral complex may be regarded as a resonance hybrid of several structures. The six π-electrons previously distributed over the six-carbon benzene skeleton are now considered distributed over only five carbons. Whether such a system complexed to a manganese(I) cation is of lower energy than one containing manganese(0) complexed to a radical hybrid containing one less electron, or whether the compound rearranges to form a *sigma*-bond to manganese, cannot be decided presently.

Although the problem may be mainly semantic (58), it would be of advantage to use a representation that would explain both the physical and the chemical properties of the compound.

The displacement of one carbonyl by a cyanide in the benzene-tricarbonyl-manganese(I) ion is another example of nucleophilic attack on the metal (12):

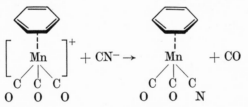

It is tempting to hypothesize that the reaction of similar salts with phenyllithium likewise occurs by nucleophilic attack on the metal with the transient formation of a *sigma*-phenyl-manganese bond. The resulting complex can then rearrange to the compound isolated, and a reasonable explanation for the first proposed *endo* configuration has been rationalized.

In this connection it is not entirely unreasonable to suggest a homolysis of the manganese-to-phenyl *sigma*-bond causing reduction of the metal and a rearrangement by phenyl-radical migration to the π-bonded benzene nucleus. The product could then be represented by a resonance hybrid involving structures such as the one shown:

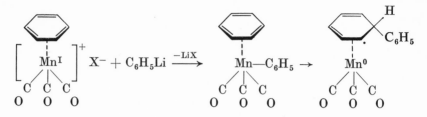

Rearrangements

Although the reactions described in the following are in essence prepa-
rations of arene-tricarbonyl-metal(0) complexes, they are discussed here
because of the similarities to those just described. The reactant, a
tropylium-tricarbonyl-chromium salt, was prepared by hydride abstraction
from cycloheptatriene-tricarbonyl-chromium(0) (74), a method previously
used for the preparation of tropylium-tricarbonyl-molybdenum(0) salts (18):

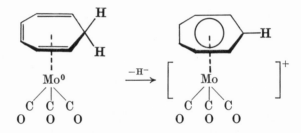

Whether the salt exemplifies the stabilization of a carbonium ion,
similar to the stabilization shown for ferrocene-type carbonium ions (4,6,49),
or whether it is another example of the stabilization of unusual aromatic
systems, cannot at present be decided.   X-ray investigation favors the latter
interpretation for cyclopentadienyl-cycloheptatrienyl-vanadium (22,58):

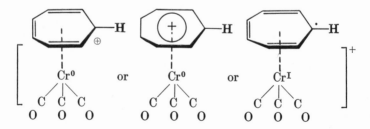

Salts of tropylium-tricarbonyl-chromium(0) undergo two types of reactions with nucleophiles depending on the character of the latter (73,74).
With nucleophiles such as cyanide, methoxide, or phenyl anions, the

products are substituted (probably *endo*) cycloheptatriene-tricarbonyl-chromium(0) compounds:

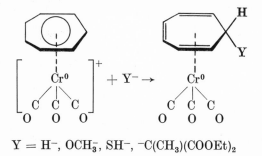

$$Y = H^-, OCH_3^-, SH^-, {}^-C(CH_3)(COOEt)_2$$

The reaction bears many similarities to that of phenyllithium with benzene-tricarbonyl-manganese(I) and may follow a similar path.

When the salt is added to excess sodium cyclopentadienide or sodiomalonic ester, a remarkable rearrangement occurs which leads to benzene-tricarbonyl-chromium(0):

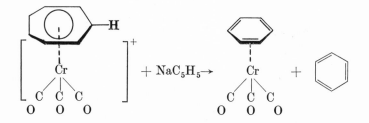

The reaction involves ring expansion and ring contraction, as was shown by experiments involving tritium-labeling or methyl substitution. It is the seven-membered ring which produces the benzene ligand, and thus, presumably, the five-membered ring which yields the free benzene molecule:

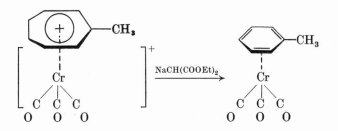

Tropylium-tricarbonyl-molybdenum(0) also undergoes the same reaction (74).

An insight into the mechanism of the reaction was achieved by the isolation of an intermediate in the reaction when inverse addition of the reactants was used:

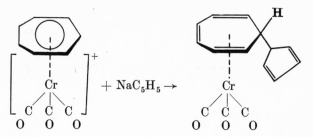

The same intermediate could be prepared in low yield by an independent but not less remarkable route:

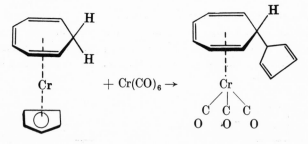

Rearrangement occurred when this intermediate was treated with a base such as sodium methoxide (or excess sodium cyclopentadienide):

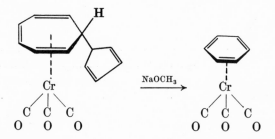

Analogous steps were demonstrated to occur when sodiomalonic ester was used:

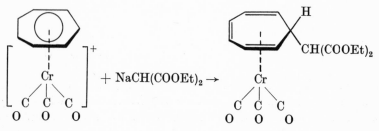

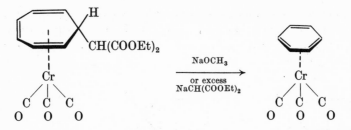

However, if, instead of sodiomalonic ester, sodiomethylmalonic ester was used, the second step did not proceed:

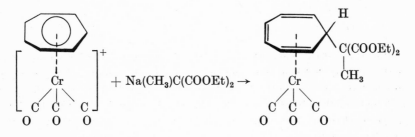

Thus the rearrangement appears to be initiated by the removal of a proton:*

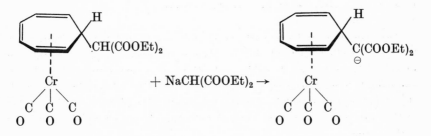

The rearrangement of the anion may be depicted as follows:

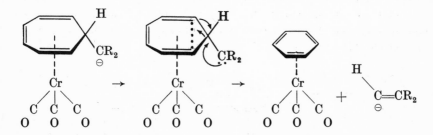

* No comment is given concerning the fact that the rearrangement does proceed all the way to benzene-tricarbonyl-chromium(O) with sodium methyl-cyclopentadienide (74).

It would be interesting to confirm this mechanism by the character-ization of the other fragment (in non-aqueous medium: $^{\ominus}CH = CR_2$). The corresponding mechanism for the reaction using sodium cyclopentadienide is then formulated:

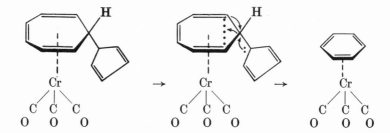

Reactions of this type which result in fundamental bond rearrangements in the carbon skeleton of polyolefinic compounds complexed to transition metals have just recently been brought to light. It is not difficult to anticipate further developments in this area that may lead to the elucidation of the mechanisms operating on synthetic or naturally occurring catalysts for related reactions.

Hydride Reduction of Manganese Complexes

The reduction of benzenoid compounds complexed to transition metals has been studied particularly in relation to mixed bis-arene-metal com-plexes. Examples of hydride reduction of mono-arene-carbonyl-metal compounds have, however, been reported (112,113). Since the evidence for the structures proposed is almost exclusively of a physicochemical nature (NMR and infrared spectra), any conclusions drawn should be considered with caution.

The reaction of cyclohexadiene-1,3 with $Mn_2(CO)_{10}$ led to the isolation of a neutral compound represented by the formula $\{C_6H_7\}Mn(CO)_3$. The same compound was obtained in better yield by reducing benzene-tricarbonyl-manganese(I) perchlorate with lithium aluminum hydride or sodium borohydride (112,113):

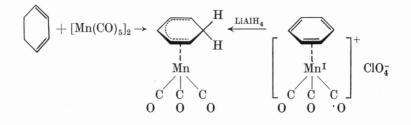

The structure of the compound having six electrons located over 5-carbon atoms may also be presented in one or more of the following ways:

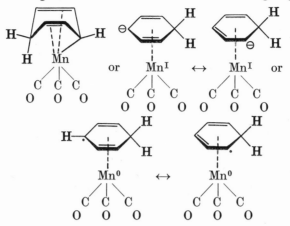

Although the main product of the hydride-reduction of the benzene-tricarbonyl-manganese(I) cation has the molecular formula $C_6H_7Mn(CO)_3$, it was later found that yet another complex, $C_6H_{8\ or\ 9}Mn(CO)_3$, could be isolated in trace amounts. It was assumed that the latter compound could not simply be a cyclohexadiene-tricarbonyl-manganese(0) (similar to the known iron, molybdenum, or cobalt complexes of this structure), since this compound would be a radical. Although the molecular weight and analyses support the formula, $C_6H_8Mn(CO)_3$, the evidence as a whole leads the authors to the tentative conclusion that the compound is the hydrido-derivative of the unknown $C_6H_8Mn(CO)_3$ despite the lack of direct evidence for a Mn—H bond (113). Two possible routes of formation are shown:

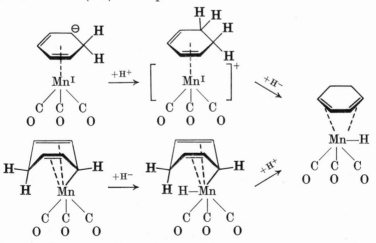

Since no nuclear magnetic- or electron spin-resonance measurements could be obtained with this compound, its structure cannot be considered as established.

Coupling of Alkynes

The products obtained from the oligomerization of alkynes at carbonyl metal centers in most cases are not arene-carbonyl-metal(0) complexes, but the benzenoid compounds themselves (1,50,51,62,63,72,106):

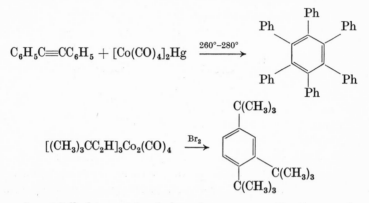

In using trialkyl- or triaryl-chromium as coordination centers for oligomerization of alkynes it was observed that under certain conditions the aryl or alkyl groups were incorporated into the resulting benzenoid products. In a somewhat analogous fashion a CO-group, previously a carbonyl ligand, often appears in the product as a keto group. Thus butyne-2 under the influence of light with pentacarbonyl-iron yields duroquinone-tricarbonyl-iron(0) (69,85,87):

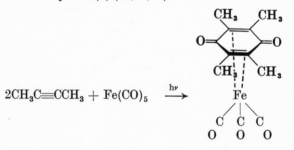

Many reactions of this type have been studied, but they will not be discussed here since they have recently been reviewed elsewhere (114). Carbonyl-metal complexes have been used also in the polymerization of dienes (82).

Decomposition

It often becomes essential in the elucidation of the structure of an arene-carbonyl-metal complex to be able to decompose it in such a way that both the number of carbonyl ligands per metal atom and the structure of the benzenoid compound can be established. This becomes especially significant in the synthesis of unusual aromatic systems at metal centers.

In many cases the complexes are sufficiently labile so that mere heating permits the recovery of the π-bonded benzenoid ligand (16). However, this method is not useful for the quantitative estimation of carbonyl ligands, nor is it useful for the recovery of unstable aromatic compounds.

A number of other methods rely on the displacement of the benzenoid ligand by other ligands. Thus triphenylphosphine (80), triphenylphosphite (71), and pyridine (76) are capable of selectively removing the arene ligand:

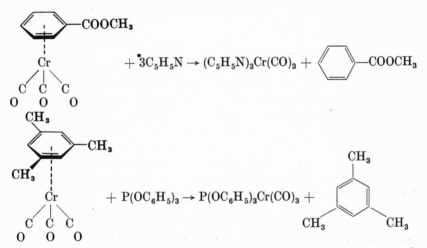

The convenient procedure of heating the complex in diglyme or the dibutylether of diethylene glycol leads to an intermediate that can be used further for the preparation of other carbonyl metal complexes (110):

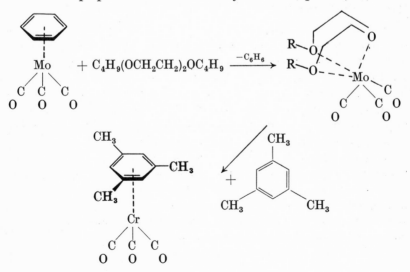

Dimethylformamide can likewise be employed in a similar procedure (10,110), and the tris-dimethylformamide of molybdenum(0) can be isolated.

For quantitative purposes decomposition by oxidative degradation is more convenient (10,76):

$$\{C_6H_6\}Cr(CO)_3 + \tfrac{3}{2} I_2 \rightarrow CrI_3 + 3\,CO + C_6H_6$$

$$[\{C_6H_5CH_3\}_3Co_3(CO)_2]I + I_2 \xrightarrow[\text{2) Mg}]{\text{1) } C_5H_5N} 2CO + 3C_6H_5CH_3$$

The arene-tricarbonyl-metal complexes are in many cases unstable toward acids (especially sulfuric acid) and can for qualitative purposes be decomposed in this way (19,85).

PHYSICAL PROPERTIES

Proposals of unusual structures or types of bonding often spur investigators to rely on physicochemical measurements to a large extent for the purpose of substantiating or rejecting the structure proposed. The suggestion that Hein's compounds were "sandwich" complexes of the ferrocene type, in which the benzenoid layers were π-bonded to the transition metal, chromium, was initially met with much skepticism. Considerable effort by theoretical chemists has been spent on attempts to understand the bonding involved in transition metal complexes of aromatic systems; yet one cannot at present claim that any one of the many approaches describes the bonding in sufficient detail to account for all the physicochemical and other experimental observations collected. In the following sections the physical properties of transition metal complexes containing one benzenoid compound and at least one carbonyl ligand will be discussed.

Magnetic Properties

Most mono-arene-carbonyl-metal complexes are diamagnetic. Despite the extensive criticism of the valence-bond approach to electron distribution in complexes, its shortcomings prompted the development of the more sophisticated crystal field and ligand field theories. The value of any theory of bonding rests not only in its capability of unifying the largest number of experimental observations in the most precise manner, but also in its capability of predicting new structures or suggesting new types of chemistry. One of the values of the valence-bond method has been its capacity to combine the concepts of the periodicity of the elements with the knowledge of the geometric and magnetic properties of a great number of complexes in a non-sophisticated system. This lends itself to simple presentations that are easily comprehended. It is not a failure of this system that has rendered it incapable of a reasonable interpretation of quantitative measurements of such properties as spectra, bond distances, and thermodynamic properties, but rather a realized but inherent short-coming of the system.

Throughout a large range of complexes good agreement was obtained between the number of unpaired electrons found and the number predicted on the basis that one arene nucleus occupies three hybrid orbitals in the valence-bond picture of d^2sp^3 hybridization for the central metal (29,37):

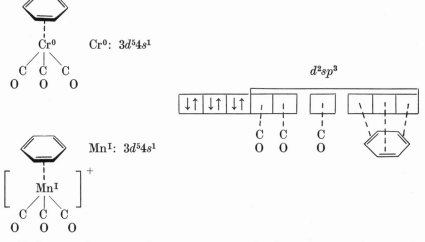

Unfortunately, magnetic measurements of other representative metals are missing. Such measurements should be particularly useful for paramagnetic complexes containing an even number of unpaired electrons because of the difficulty in obtaining information from nuclear magnetic resonance spectra or triplet-state electron spin-resonance spectra.

Dipole Moments

Arene-tricarbonyl-metal complexes are uniquely suited as models for studying the influence of substituents on the dipole moments of compounds having π-bonds from a benzenoid nucleus to metals. The relatively easy preparation of an extensive series of compounds has induced three independent groups to study their dipole moments (38,83,97,99). Compounds of the type {arene}Cr(CO)$_2$L likewise are accessible and well suited for the same measurements.

In bis-arene-metal(0) complexes a polarization in the direction of the metal from one ring is compensated by a similar polarization from the other ring. In "unsymmetrical" complexes, such as the ones under discussion, the theoretical possibility still exists that the group on one side may provide a partial component along the molecular axis of equal magnitude and opposite direction to that provided by the groups on the other side. This is an unusual case, and normally the partial moments are different and contribute in either parallel or antiparallel directions. It follows that when a moment is observed for a complex, one of these situations exists. It is reasonable to assume that large moments correspond to the situation in which the partial moments add (are pointed in the same direction) although this, of course, is not necessarily so.

Arene-Carbonyl-Metal Complexes. The dipole moments of arene-tricarbonyl-chromium(0) complexes are large; and, in general, electron-releasing substituents on the benzenoid group increase the dipole moment relative to benzene-tricarbonyl-chromium(0), while electron-attracting groups decrease the total moment. This effect agrees with the axial component of the bond moments pointing from the arene towards the metal and that of the combined carbonyl-metal either pointing towards the metal and being smaller than the other one (case 2) or pointing in the same direction as the other component (case 1):

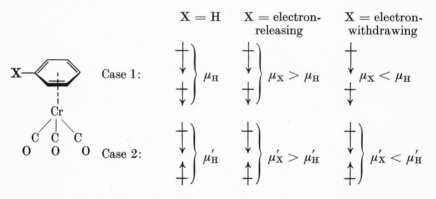

The dipole moments of some representative compounds are given in Table 3–1.

The decision between the two existing possibilities, case 1 and case 2, was made mainly on the basis of arguments resting on the shift in infrared C—O frequency in the compounds as a function of the substituent on the arene. This effect is discussed later in greater detail. Suffice it to say here that the C—O frequency is dependent on the extent of back-donation from the metal. A pictorial representation of one M—CO group in valence-bond language is given by A and B, in which it is imagined that the two electrons constituting the π-portion of the M—C bond in structure B originate from the metal:

$$M^{\ominus}\!\!-\!\!C\!\!\equiv\!\!O^{\oplus}: \qquad\qquad M\!\!=\!\!C\!\!=\!\!\overset{\cdot}{O}:$$
$$\phantom{M^{\ominus}}AB$$

In terms of group moments, the resonance structure A would contribute in the sense of case 2, whereas structure B would have little or no effect. In carbonyl-metal complexes both these limiting structures should be considered and, depending on which one predominates, the magnitude of the combined carbonyl-metal partial moment would vary, but always be directed towards the metal. The greater contribution of structure A would increase the group moment toward the metal relative to structure B. One may consider, to a first approximation, that if structure A is favored, a strengthening of the carbon-oxygen bond would result. A change in C—O bond

TABLE 3–I

Dipole Moments of Arene-Tricarbonyl-Chromium(0) Complexes

Compound	Dipole Moment (D)	Solvent	Reference
$\{C_6H_6\}Cr(CO)_3$	4.92 ± 0.05	Benzene	38
$\{CH_3C_6H_5\}Cr(CO)_3$	5.20 ± 0.04	Benzene	38
$\{p\text{-}(CH_3)_2C_6H_4\}Cr(CO)_3$	5.39 ± 0.05	Benzene	38
$\{1,3,5\text{-}(CH_3)_3C_6H_3\}Cr(CO)_3$	5.56 ± 0.06	Benzene	38
$\{(CH_3)_6C_6\}Cr(CO)_3$	6.22 ± 0.02	Benzene	38
$\{HOC_6H_5\}Cr(CO)_3$	5.13 ± 0.07	Benzene	38
$\{FC_6H_5\}Cr(CO)_3$	4.75 ± 0.03	Benzene	38
$\{CH_3OOCC_6H_5\}Cr(CO)_3$	4.47 ± 0.03	Benzene	38
$\{C_6H_6\}Cr(CO)_3$	4.38	Heptane	83
$\{CH_3C_6H_5\}Cr(CO)_3$	4.70	Heptane	83
$\{p\text{-}F_2C_6H_4\}Cr(CO)_3$	3.97	Heptane	83
$\{p\text{-}Cl_2C_6H_4\}Cr(CO)_3$	3.72	Heptane	83

order from 3 in structure A to 2 in structure B can be recognized by a shift in the infrared C—O stretching mode to a lower frequency, paralleling a decrease in force constant of the C—O bond.

In arene-tricarbonyl-metal complexes the frequency of the carbonyl stretching mode is dependent upon the substituent on the arene. It is considered that an electron-releasing substituent on the arene increases the electron density on the metal and consequently increases the extent of back-donation to the carbonyl group, structure B. This should cause a decrease in the C—O frequency. Or, conversely, a decrease in C—O frequency must have been caused by the larger contribution of structure B, which in turn is the result of the higher electron density on the metal arising from the electron-releasing substituent on the arene. A greater contribution of structure B would promote a decrease in the opposing moment component directed toward the metal and increase the total moment of the complex.

The general trends were observed to be those mentioned, and some attempts have been made to correlate Hammett's *sigma* values with the experimentally observed dipole moments. Qualitatively, a correlation might be expected to exist, since aromatic substituents may be classified as electron donor or acceptors on the basis of the sign of the *sigma* value. However, quantitative correlation should be viewed with caution because the *sigma* values were derived relative to a given reaction taking place at a certain position relative to the substituent. Moreover, substituents would drastically affect the electron density at the various positions in the aromatic nucleus, and thus the symmetry of the wave functions presumed to be involved in the bonding to the metal.

General rules were set forth showing a colligative increase in dipole moment with increasing number of substituents (83); accordingly, axial contributions for CH_3, OCH_3, $N(CH_3)_2$, C_6H_5, H, Cl, and F substituents were derived. On the basis of these it was concluded that neither the resonance nor the inductive effects alone, but rather the combined electronic effects of the substituents were governing the changes in dipole moments observed. Accordingly, a linear relationship was found to exist between the sum, $\sigma_I + \sigma_{R'}$ and $\Delta\mu_X$ (the shift in dipole moment of benzene-tricarbonyl-chromium(0) by the substituent X).

The effect of solvent on the dipole moment of such complexes was demonstrated by a change in dipole moment of benzene-tricarbonyl-chromium(0) from 4.31 D in cyclohexane to 5.33 D in dioxane (93). This increase was assumed to be due to the capability of a benzene molecule, when π-bonded to a metal, to accept electrons from a donor-type solvent; the benzene molecule has been changed from a nucleophile to an electrophile:

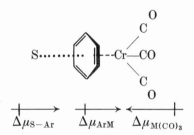

Later it was shown that the solvent-dependence of substituted benzene-tricarbonyl-chromium(0) complexes likewise was dependent on the substituent (2,94). The acceptor strength of the benzene molecule should be increased by electron-withdrawing substituents and decreased by electron-releasing groups. This general trend is observed experimentally: electron-releasing groups increase the dipole moment and electron-withdrawing substituents decrease it. However, the solvent had an effect not only on the absolute magnitude of the dipole moments, but also on the change in dipole moment caused by the substitution of one group for another. In general, the magnitude of the dipole moment decreases along the solvent series: dioxane $> C_6H_6 >$ heptane (94). An electron-repelling substituent causes a smaller change in the better donor solvent than in the poorer one. This appears to be in accord with the postulate that the benzenoid portion acts as an acceptor for donor solvents. Electron-releasing groups, Y, would decrease the acceptor strength of the benzenoid compound, whereas electron attracting groups, X, would enhance this acceptor strength:

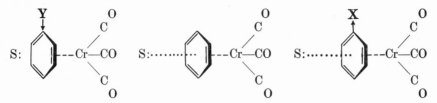

Arene-Carbonyl-Metal Complexes Containing Other Ligands. A more detailed study of the dipole moments of a large number of complexes of the general formulas $M(CO)_5L$, $M(CO)_4L_2$, {arene}$M(CO)_3$, and {arene}$M(CO)_2L$ in a variety of solvents permitted calculation of bond moments for arene—M, M—CO, and M—L (63,99).

Experimentally the total dipole moments of the compounds were measured, and the bond moments were calculated under the two assumptions that the interatomic distances do not change on substitution and that the separate groups do not influence each other (63,97). The influence of the donor molecules L on the bond moment for arene—M and especially on the bond moment for M—L were of interest in establishing the extent of back-donation from the metal to L. The moment for the M—L bond can readily be calculated for octahedral complexes $M(CO)_5L$ because the experimentally observed moment is the vectorial sum of the M—CO and L group moments and the M—L bond moment:

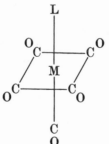

A decrease in total dipole moment was considered to be caused by an increase in back-donation to L. However, it was found on the basis of this criterion that the groups L which had the largest apparent extent of back-donation were also the ones which formed the weakest bonds in {arene} $M(CO)_2L$. Since this could not be so, it was concluded that a decrease in M—L bond moment could be caused either by an increase in extent of back-donation or by a decrease in the strength of the *sigma*-bond.

Ligands which give preferential *cis* configuration in $L_2M(CO)_4$ are generally considered less likely to accept electrons from the metal by back-donation than those which favor *trans* configuration. For the former type of ligand, a decrease in the M—L bond moment can be caused only by a weakening of the *sigma*-bond to the metal. If the ligand can accept electrons by back-donation from the metal, a decrease in bond moment can be the result of either of two effects: the opposing contribution caused by back-donation or the primary weakening of the *sigma*-bond.

It has previously been mentioned that a lowering of the C—O infrared frequency in $\{ArX\}Cr(CO)_3$ parallels the donation of electron from the benzenoid compound:

$$\text{For } \{p\text{-}(CH_3OOC)_2C_6H_4\}Cr(CO)_3, \ \nu_{CO} \ (cm^{-1}) = 1990$$

$$\text{For } \{C_6H_6\}Cr(CO)_3, \ \nu_{CO} = 1975$$

$$\text{For } \{p\text{-}(CH_3)_2C_6H_4\}Cr(CO)_3, \ \nu_{CO} = 1965$$

This effect indicates that Cr=C=O structures are favored for compounds in which the substituents are electron-releasing. The preponderance of the Cr=C=O over the $Cr^{\ominus}$—$C\equiv O^{\oplus}$ would cause a decrease in the group moment for $Cr(CO)_3$, opposed to the group moment for $\{arene\}Cr$. The total effect would be a decrease in the dipole moment of the complex. However, in the calculation of the group moment for the $\{arene\}Cr$ component, the assumption had been made that the group moment for the $Cr(CO)_3$ component did not change with substitution on the arene. Since this assumption led to incorrect conclusions concerning the stability of the Cr—L bond in $\{arene\}Cr(CO)_2L$ complexes, it became necessary to correct the partial moments for the $\{arene\}Cr$ group for the change in the $Cr(CO)_3$ component, a change which could be confirmed by a shift in the infrared C—O frequencies.

It was particularly significant to establish whether the M—L bond component likewise varied with the substituent on the arene. Such a change was observed, but in the opposite direction to that expected: larger bond moments were calculated for M—L if the substituents on the arene were changed from electron-attracting to electron-releasing. Increased back-donation to the ligand L and less favorable donation of L to the metal (because of increased electron density on the metal) both should have decreased the bond moment for M—L, which is opposed to that of the $\{arene\}M$ bond moment. Which effect dominated should have been dependent on the capability of the donor ligand to accept back-donation from the metal. The observed discrepancy was explained in terms of the reluctance of some ligands to accommodate the excess charge on the metal by back-donation. This requires a further increase in back-donation to the remaining carbonyl, and thus a decrease in the partial moment for the $M(CO)_2$ group, especially for electron-releasing arenes. Since this alteration was not taken into account in calculating the contribution of the M—L group to the total dipole moment, the discrepancy had arisen. By this reasoning it would be expected that for compounds containing a ligand L incapable of accepting back-donation, the C—O frequency should decrease more rapidly in the compounds:

$$\{p\text{-}(CH_3OOC)_2C_6H_4\}Cr(CO)_2L > \{C_6H_6\}Cr(CO)_2L > \{(CH_3)_6C_6\}Cr(CO)_2L$$

than in the corresponding tricarbonyl series. The values observed were $1925 > 1892 > 1845 \, (cm^{-1})$ for L = piperidine and $1990 > 1975 > 1950$ for the corresponding {arene}Cr(CO)$_3$ complexes (98). It was confirmed also that the shift in the C—O frequency was less pronounced for ligands, L, which were capable of accepting back-donation. Thus, for the same series of {arene}Cr(CO)$_2$L having L = $(CH_3)_2SO$, the frequencies were 1936, 1908, 1878.

Spectra

Infrared. Infrared spectra of arene complexes containing carbonyl ligands have been used widely in interpreting bonding forces and the symmetry of the arene ligand. Several pertinent reviews dealing with infrared spectra of inorganic complexes have appeared recently (14,42,52) in which the problems related to theoretical interpretation have been discussed in detail. A general discussion of this type is beyond the purpose of this treatise. Therefore, only the recent comprehensive studies on the use of infrared spectroscopy particularly as applied to arene-carbonyl-metal complexes will be mentioned.

The effect of back-donation should be kept in mind in considering carbonyl ligand absorption. One way of looking at the shift in the C—O stretching frequency is to regard the position of the absorption (which in an isolated system is proportional to the square root of the force constant) as a function of the bond order of the C—O linkage. In free carbon monoxide the bond order is highest, almost 3, and the C—O stretch band appears at $2150 \, cm^{-1}$. In carbonyl ligands the bond order is lowered, depending on the extent of back-donation from the metal to the carbon atom (bond order between 3 and 2), causing absorption near $2000 \, cm^{-1}$. A carbonyl group present in conjugated organic molecules or as a bridging group may be considered to have bond orders of 2 or less (1700–$1600 \, cm^{-1}$), whereas the C—O stretching absorption in compounds such as ethers (with bond orders of $ca.$ 1) appears near $1100 \, cm^{-1}$.

Analysis by normal coordinates of the C—O valence vibrations in arene-tricarbonyl-metal compounds was discouraging because of the complicated structure of the complex (45). Hence an empirical method was applied to assign the M—C vibrations which in pure carbonyl-metal(0) compounds appear in the range of 300–$600 \, cm^{-1}$. It was found that the sum of the wave numbers for two absorptions, one of which corresponded to the C—O frequency, for an extended series of carbonyl-metal complexes, gave a constant value. If one assumes direct proportionality between bond order and frequency, then it is reasonable to assign the other absorption to M—C vibrations (less so than to a M—C—O deformation). This is so inasmuch as the bond-order decrease in the C—O bond would parallel a bond-order increase for the M—C bond:

$$^\ominus M\!-\!C\!\equiv\!O^\oplus \leftrightarrow M\!=\!C\!=\!O \leftrightarrow {}^\oplus M\!\equiv\!C\!-\!O^\ominus$$

A detailed study (43) of the infrared spectrum of $\{C_6H_6\}Cr(CO)_3$ and $\{C_6D_6\}Cr(CO)_3$ is based on the assumption that the complex does not have a three-fold axis of symmetry (13). In order to establish the symmetry properties of the arene group, a normal coordinate analysis was attempted. A striking similarity to the assignment in bis-benzene-chromium(0) was noted, and this aided the separation of skeletal and $Cr(CO)_3$ modes, as did the comparison of the spectra of $\{C_6H_6\}Cr(CO)_3$ and $\{C_6D_6\}Cr(CO)_3$. A comparison of the vibrations expected from the selection rules with those found gave rise to the conclusion that the benzene molecule has local C_{3v} symmetry whether the complex was present in a crystal, in solution, or in the vapor state. This led to the consideration that the benzene molecule when complexed to $Cr(CO)_3$ should be considered as fixed in one Kekulé structure. This conclusion is not in accord with the latest findings from X-ray crystallography measurements, which showed no pronounced alteration in bond lengths within the experimental error (15,54); and microwave spectra showed that the molecule was a symmetrical top (109), excluding a distinction between C_{6v} or C_{3v} symmetry of the main axis. Analogous interpretations of the spectra of $\{C_6H_6\}Mo(CO)_3$ and $\{C_6D_6\}Mo(CO)_3$ likewise afforded C_{3v} to the symmetry of the benzene ring (44).

Certain intensity changes were noted in complexing various benzenoid compounds to tricarbonyl-chromium(0) as a group (53). This empirical treatment is valuable in determining characteristic changes which appear when a free benzenoid compound becomes π-bonded to a metal. Three pronounced changes were found to occur on complexing (53):

1. The aromatic C—H modes merge into one band with a pronounced decrease in intensity.
2. The 1600 and 1500 bands, generally attributed to skeletal C—C stretching modes, are shifted from their normal position by 25–100 cm^{-1} and 30–40 cm^{-1} toward lower energy. In addition, the appearance of a strong band at 1390 cm^{-1} for alkyl-substituted arene-tricarbonyl-chromium(0) was noted.
3. Non-complexed aromatic compounds usually show very intense bands in the 850–670 cm^{-1} region, the so-called C—H out-of-plane vibrations. These bands, often used for assignment of substitution, are missing in the spectra of the π-complexes. Instead, one weak absorption (ca. one-tenth the apparent molar absorptivity) in the range 820–795 cm^{-1} may be seen.

This absorption is independent of substitution on the aromatic nucleus (exceptions: p-xylene- and methyl benzoate-tricarbonyl-chromium(0) show two bands). In the far infrared region two intense bands in the 620–600 cm^{-1} region and two more at 530 and 475 cm^{-1} are tentatively assigned to C—O bending and Cr—C stretching vibrations.

The carbonyl region is very characteristic: two intense bands at *ca.* 1990 and 1920 cm^{-1} are almost always present. These two bands are shown by most complexes having the tricarbonyl metal moiety (40):

$$\{C_6H_6\}Cr(CO)_3, \quad [C_5H_5Cr(CO)_3]^-, \quad (NH_3)_3Cr(CO)_3, \quad C_5H_5Mn(CO)_3$$

Several independent studies (2,40,98) show that C—O frequencies shift to lower values when the electron density on the aromatic nucleus is increased. The range for the monosubstituted $\{$arene-X$\}$Cr(CO)$_3$ for the high frequency band extends from 1997 cm^{-1} in methyl-benzoate-tricarbonyl-chromium(0) to 1969 cm^{-1} for dimethyl aniline-tricarbonyl-chromium(0) (the low frequency band likewise undergoes a parallel decrease). From a comparison between 1,2-, 1,3,5-, and 1,2,4,5-methyl-substituted benzene complexes it was apparent that the 1,3,5-substitution did not render the bond between the arene and the metal exceptionally stable as had been postulated previously (27). More surprising is the observation that the band position and shift on substitution is insensitive to the central metal in a homologous series benzene-tricarbonyl-chromium(0), -molybdenum(0), and -tungsten(0). This suggests that electronic effects are transferred equally well *via* the three metals.

In a series of benzene- and cyclopentadienyl-carbonyl-metal complexes the changes in half-widths and extinction coefficient (41) were interpreted to mean that an increase in bond order causes a decrease in C—O bond moment and also a decrease in transition moment of vibration. Expressed differently: as the frequency of the C—O stretching mode increases, as for instance for the pair $\{C_6H_6\}Cr(CO)_3$; $C_5H_5Mn(CO)_3$ with ν_{CO} (cm^{-1}) at 1987, 2035, the integrated extinction value decreases markedly (11.1 × 10^{-7} to 7.3 × 10^{-7}).

A plot of observed dipole moments of arene-tricarbonyl-metal(0) complexes *versus* the wave number of the C—O frequency produced a straight line. In considering the effect of a 0.2 D increase in dipole moment per methyl substituent, it was rationalized that the increase in charge transfer per methyl substituent over the ring to metal distance would not suffice, and that the charge was further separated by back-donation to the carbonyl ligands. There is, however, a significantly shorter over-all Cr—O distance in hexacarbonyl-chromium(0) than in benzene-tricarbonyl-chromium(0) (13). The quantitative treatment of the relation between dipole moment and C—O frequency, which appeared after methods for the calculation of bond moments were developed (93,94,96,99), has been discussed in connection with dipole-moment measurements. Experience with arene-tricarbonyl-metal complexes led to an extended study of the back-donation in complexes of the type {arene}Cr(CO)$_2$L. Here the electronic influence on the arene may either be transferred exclusively to the carbonyl if L is incapable of π-bonding or, if such bonding is possible, to both L- and the carbonyl-ligands. This study permitted the arrangement of donor ligands in a series with decreasing π-acceptor characteristics (98): CO > isonitrile $\sim$ (CH$_3$)$_2$SO $\sim$ PR$_3$ $\gg$ nitrile > pyridine. Practical experience had demonstrated that stability characteristics led to a similar series and promoted the thought that a decrease in extent of π-bonding by back-donation labilized the Cr—L bond. The disconcerting observation that isonitrile complexes were very much less stable than the corresponding PR$_3$ complex and the fact that the total apparent bond moments for the Cr—N and Cr—P compounds differed by *ca.* 1 Debye unit forced the conclusion that the *sigma*-bond contribution to the bond moment is lowered for the donors having the lower polarizability. It thus became apparent that the lability of a ligand L in a complex {arene}Cr(CO)$_2$L is primarily a function of the polarity of the *sigma*-bond, while back-donation (either d_π—d_π or d_π—p_π) is only an additional contributor to the total bond strength. The revised ligand-chromium stability row appears as follows:

	CrCO	>	Cr(PR$_3$)	$\simeq$	Cr[SO(CH$_3$)$_2$]	>
σ-contribution	large		large			
π-contribution	large		medium			

	Cr-(quinoline)	>	Cr(CNR)	>	Cr(NCR)	$\simeq$	CrNR$_3$
	large		medium		medium		large
	small		medium		small		none

Ultraviolet. Ultraviolet spectra have been recorded in a number of instances (8,25,35). In general, three absorptions are quoted in the regions: 218–221, 251–264 (shoulder), and 315–324 mμ with log ε of 4.4, 3.8, and 3.2, respectively. No efforts have been made to interpret these transitions, although from analogies to other carbonyl-metal complexes it appears that the absorptions below 300 mμ are due to the carbonyl moieties (64).

Nuclear Magnetic Resonance. Nuclear magnetic resonance, which has proved a valuable tool in the study of transitions from σ-allylic- to π-allylic-transition metal compounds has rarely been used in arene-tricarbonyl chemistry (61,107). The ring protons appear at higher field strength than in free benzenoid compounds, since the aromatic ring current is perturbed by π-bond formation to the metal (98). The observation of a dependence of dipole moment on solvent could also be transferred to nuclear magnetic spectra. The effect was most pronounced for benzene-tricarbonyl-chromium(0). The benzene nucleus in this compound appears to have the largest acceptor tendency for donor solvents. Its protons should be the least influenced by ring current, and their chemical shift should appear the furthest removed from those of free benzene, as is indeed the case.

For p-disubstituted π-bonded benzenoid compounds, the protons *ortho* to electron-withdrawing groups experience smaller shifts to higher fields than do the *meta* protons (61). In general, of the four possible coupling constants that can exist between two identical spin pairs, the one between the protons in the *ortho* position experiences the most pronounced lowering on π-bonding (from 8.8–7.8 to 6.8–6.4).

For complexes belonging to the same isoelectronic family (114) having the same π-bonded arene, namely {arene}Cr(CO)$_3$, {arene}Mo(CO)$_3$, and {arene}W(CO)$_3$, the lowering of the ortho-coupling constants is 1.4, 1.2, and 1.5 cps, respectively, a change which is thought to exceed that caused by a change in the π-electron participation. The change is hence attributed to an alteration in the σ-bonds of the aromatic nucleus. That {arene} Mo(CO)$_3$ constitutes an exception is also demonstrated by the chemical shifts of the ring protons for {p-xylene}M(CO)$_3$. For M = Cr, Mo, W these are 4.74, 4.37, and 4.55, respectively.

Although not strictly relevant, a remark concerning the high-resolution nuclear magnetic resonance spectra of compounds of the structure cyclohexadienyl-tricarbonyl-manganese(I) (113) is appropriate:

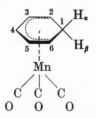

This compound shows three types of hydrogen atoms (shifts in τ units relative to tetramethylsilane): (A) at 4.80 τ a triplet due to H$_{(4)}$ split by H$_{(3)}$ and H$_{(5)}$, and by H$_{(2)}$ and H$_{(6)}$; (B) at 5.84 τ due to H$_{(3)}$ and H$_{(5)}$, split appropriately by H$_{(4)}$ and the H$_{(2)}$ and H$_{(6)}$ protons; (C) at 7.65 τ, assigned to H$_{(2)}$ and H$_{(6)}$; this is complex and overlaps with that for the protons of the CH$_2$ group; H$_\beta$ and H$_\alpha$ at 7.5 τ and 8.44 τ, respectively, split each other mutually (11 cps) and are further split by H$_{(2)}$ and H$_{(6)}$. Since the latter is absent in {C$_6$H$_6$D}Mn(CO)$_3$, this is assigned to the H$_\beta$ proton. It is perhaps significant to note that the appreciable solvent shift for these compounds and π-allylmetal complexes (20) in polar solvents may be due to the same effect as that observed in the dependence of dipole moment on solvent (94).

Recently a revision of the interpretation of the NMR data for substituted cyclohexadienyl complexes has appeared (57), demonstrating the caution with which one should proceed in the interpretation of the NMR spectra of such complexes.   An X-ray structure analysis of a phenyl-substituted cyclopentadienyl-cobalt complex had shown that the phenyl group was in an *exo* position to the metal (11).   Arguments based mainly on NMR data had previously led to the conclusion that an *endo*-substituent was present in similar cyclohexadienyl complexes (56,113).

The more definite demonstration of the presence of a hydrido-ligand to a transition metal (19) should be kept in mind, whenever such ligands are suspected.   By using a number of strong acids, it was shown that a variety of {arene}Cr(CO)$_3$ complexes were protonated on the metal, presumably, by the appearance of a broad high-field line ($\tau_{M-H} = 12$–14) in the NMR spectra of the otherwise unisolable compounds:

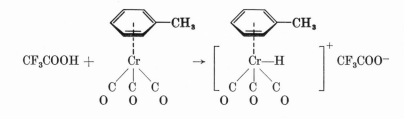

TABLE 3–2

Arene-Carbonyl-Metal Complexes

Formula	M.P. (°C)	References (Chapter 3)
$\{C_6H_6\}Cr(CO)_3$	162–163	33, 34, 77, 79, 80
$\{C_6H_5F\}Cr(CO)_3$	122.5–124	80
$\{C_6H_5Cl\}Cr(CO)_3$	102–103	34, 55, 80, 81
$\{C_6H_5NH_2\}Cr(CO)_3$	160	34, 76, 79, 80, 81
$\{C_6H_5OH\}Cr(CO)_3$	95–96	76
	113–115	
$\{1,4\text{-}F_2C_6H_4\}Cr(CO)_3$	111	90
$\{1,4\text{-}Cl_2C_6H_4\}Cr(CO)_3$	88	90
$\{C_6H_5CH_3\}Cr(CO)_3$	82.5–83.5	34, 48, 77, 79, 80
$\{C_6H_5CH_2OH\}Cr(CO)_3$	95.5–96.5	76, 80
$\{C_6H_5OCH_3\}Cr(CO)_3$	86–87	34, 55, 80
$\{C_6H_5COOH\}Cr(CO)_3$		34, 76
$\{C_6H_5NHCH_3\}Cr(CO)_3$	122.5–124	80
$\{1\text{-}CH_3\text{-}2\text{-}NH_2C_6H_4\}Cr(CO)_3$	130–131.8	80
$\{1\text{-}CH_3\text{-}3\text{-}NH_2C_6H_4\}Cr(CO)_3$	137–138.7	80
$\{1\text{-}CH_3\text{-}4\text{-}NH_2C_6H_4\}Cr(CO)_3$	156–157.5	80
$\{1,2\text{-}(CH_3)_2C_6H_4\}Cr(CO)_3$	88–90	34, 77, 80
	90–91.4	
$\{1,3\text{-}(CH_3)_2C_6H_4\}Cr(CO)_3$	104–105	34
	103–104	77
	107–108.5	80
$\{1,4\text{-}(CH_3)_2C_6H_4\}Cr(CO)_3$	97–98	34
	98–99	77
	99–100	80
$\{C_6H_5N(CH_3)_2\}Cr(CO)_3$	142–143	76
	145.8–146.5	79, 80, 81
$\{C_6H_5CH_2COOH\}Cr(CO)_3$	190	79
$\{C_6H_5OOCCH_3\}Cr(CO)_3$	92–93	76, 79
$\{C_6H_5COOCH_3\}Cr(CO)_3$	95	34
	97.5–98.5	79, 80
$\{C_6H_5NHCOCH_3\}Cr(CO)_3$	165–169	81
	133–134	55, 76
$\{C_6H_5COCH_3\}Cr(CO)_3$	91–92.5	24, 80, 84
$\{1\text{-}CH_3\text{-}2\text{-}CH_3OC_6H_4\}Cr(CO)_3$	75–77	80
$\{1\text{-}CH_3\text{-}4\text{-}CH_3OC_6H_4\}Cr(CO)_3$	53–53.5	80
$\{1\text{-}CH_3O\text{-}4\text{-}(HOOC)C_6H_4\}Cr(CO)_3$	147–148	65
$[\{1\text{-}CH_3O\text{-}4\text{-}(OOC)C_6H_4\}Cr(CO)_3]$ brucine salt		65
$\{1,3,5\text{-}(CH_3)_3C_6H_3\}Cr(CO)_3$	177–178	79
	172–174	34, 55, 80, 81
$\{C_9H_8\}Cr(CO)_3$ indene		30, 60
$\{1\text{-}CH_3\text{-}2\text{-}N(CH_3)_2C_6H_4\}Cr(CO)_3$	76.5–78	80
$\{1\text{-}CH_3\text{-}x\text{-}(CH_3CO)C_6H_4\}Cr(CO)_3$		84
$\{1\text{-}CH_3\text{-}4\text{-}CH_3COC_6H_4\}Cr(CO)_3$	107	48
$\{1\text{-}CH_3O\text{-}3\text{-}CH_3OOCC_6H_4\}Cr(CO)_3$	57–58	65
$\{1,4\text{-}CH_3C_6H_4CH(CH_3)_2\}Cr(CO)_3$		68
$\{(CH_3)_3CC_6H_5\}Cr(CO)_3$		80
$\{C_{10}H_8\}Cr(CO)_3$ naphthalene	120d	34, 76

TABLE 3–2 (continued)

Formula	M.P. (°C)	References (Chapter 3)
$\{C_{10}H_{12}\}Cr(CO)_3$	114–115	77
tetralin	116–117	79, 80
$\{C_6H_5CH_2COOC_2H_5\}Cr(CO)_3$	oil	80
$\{1,4\text{-}(CH_3OOC)_2C_6H_4\}Cr(CO)_3$	128	93
$\{1,4\text{-}(HOCH_2CH_2OOC)_2C_6H_4\}Cr(CO)_3$	137	93
$\{(CH_3)_6C_6\}Cr(CO)_3$	232	34
	211–213	80
$\{C_{12}H_{18}\}Cr(CO)_3$	175	60
acenaphthylene		
$\{C_{13}H_{10}\}Cr(CO)_3$	138–139	30
fluorene		
$\{C_{18}H_{14}\}Cr(CO)_3$	209	39
diphenylfulvene		
$\{(C_6H_5)_4C_5O\}Cr(CO)_3$	192–196	3
tetraphenylcyclopentenone		
$\{C_{14}H_{10}\}Cr(CO)_3$	189–192	31, 111
anthracene		
$\{C_{14}H_{12}\}Cr(CO)_3$	143–145	31
dihydroanthracene		
$\{C_{14}H_{10}\}Cr(CO)_3$	157–160	31, 60
phenanthrene		
$\{C_{18}H_{12}\}Cr(CO)_3$		31
chrysene		
$\{C_{16}H_{10}\}Cr(CO)_3$		60
pyrene		
$\{C_{16}H_{14}\}Cr(CO)_3$		5, 67
1,4-diphenylbutadiene		
$\{C_{16}H_{14}\}Cr_2(CO)_6$	174–176	5
1,4-diphenylbutadiene		
$[\{C_{16}H_{14}\}Cr_2(CO)_6]Fe(CO)_3$	191–193	5
1,4-diphenylbutadiene		
$[\{C_{16}H_{14}\}Cr(CO)_3]Fe(CO)_3$	170d	67
1,4-diphenylbutadiene	186–188	5
$\{C_6H_5\}\text{—}\{C_6H_5\}[Cr(CO)_3]_2$	215–216	23
$\{C_6H_5\}\text{—}NH\text{—}\{C_6H_5\}[Cr(CO)_3]_2$	210–212	23
$\{C_6H_5\}\text{—}CH_2\text{—}\{C_6H_5\}[Cr(CO)_3]_2$	216–217	23, 16
$\{trans\text{-}C_6H_5CHCHC_6H_5\}Cr(CO)_3$	131–132	3, 23
$\{C_6H_5CH_2CH_2C_6H_5\}Cr(CO)_3$	98–100	3, 23
$\{1,1\text{-}(C_6H_5)_2CHCH_3\}Cr(CO)_3$	70	16
$\{C_6H_5\}(CH_2)_3C_6H_5Cr(CO)_3$	75	16
$C_6H_5(CH_2)_4\{C_6H_5\}Cr(CO)_3$	52	16

$$\begin{array}{c} \lceil\text{—}\{p\text{-}C_6H_4\}\text{—}\rceil \\ (CH_2)_m \qquad (CH_2)_nCr(CO)_3 \\ \lfloor\text{—}p\text{-}C_6H_4\text{—}\rfloor \end{array}$$

m	n		
2	2	253	16
2	3	125	16

TABLE 3–2 (continued)

Formula	M.P. (°C)	References (Chapter 3)
3 4	148	16
4 4	240	16
4 5	129	16
4 6	117	16
5 5	148	16
5 6	136	16
6 6	117	16
1 8	145	16
1 9	166	16
1 10	135	16
1 11	138	16
1 12	129	16
9 9	121	16
10 10	149	16
12 12	133	16

$$\begin{array}{c} \lceil\;\{p\text{-}C_6H_4\}\;\rceil \\ (CH_2)_m \qquad (CH_2)_n[Cr(CO)_3]_2 \\ \lfloor\;\{p\text{-}C_6H_4\}\;\rfloor \end{array}$$

m n		
4 5	275	16
6 6	290	16
$[\{C_6H_6\}Mn^I(CO)_3]^+[AlCl_4]^-$		112
$[\{C_6H_6\}Mn^I(CO)_3]^+[ClO_4]^-$		113
$[\{C_6H_5CH_3\}Mn^I(CO)_3]^+[ClO_4]^-$		113
$[\{1,3,5\text{-}(CH_3)_3C_6H_3\}Mn^I(CO)_3]^+I^-$		12
$[\{1,3,5\text{-}(CH_3)_3C_6H_3\}Mn^I(CO)_3]^+[ClO_4]^-$		113
$[\{C_{10}H_8\}Mn(CO)_3]^+[ClO_4]^-$ naphthalene		113
$[\{(CH_3)_6C_6\}Mn^I(CO)_3]^+[Cr(NH_3)_2(SCN)_4]^-$		113
$\{C_6H_{12}O_2\}Fe(CO)_3$ duroquinone		69, 85
$[\{1,4\text{-}(C_2H_3)_2C_6H_4\}Fe_2(CO)_6$ p-divinylbenzene		67
$\{1,3\text{-}(C_2H_3)_2C_6H_4\}Fe_2(CO)_6$ m-divinylbenzene		67
$\{C_{14}H_{10}\}Fe(CO)_3$ anthracene	140d	66
$\{C_{16}H_{12}O\}Fe(CO)_3$ 9-acetylanthracene	135	66
$\{1\text{-}CH_2CHC_{10}H_9\}Fe(CO)_3$ 1-vinylnaphthalene		66
$\{C_{12}H_8\}Fe_2(CO)_6$ acenaphthylene	158	60
$[\{C_6H_6\}_3Co_3(CO)_2]^+Br^-$		10
$[\{C_6H_6\}_3Co_3(CO)_2]^+ClO_4$		26
$[\{C_6H_6\}_3Co_3(CO)_2]^+[Co(CO)_4]^-$		10
$[\{C_6H_6\}_3Co_3(CO)_2]^+[B(C_6H_5)_4]^-$		10

TABLE 3–2 (continued)

Formula	M.P. (°C)	References (Chapter 3)
$[\{C_6H_5CH_3\}_3Co_3(CO)_2]^+Br^-$		10
$[\{C_6H_5CH_3\}_3Co_3(CO)_2]^+I^-$		10
$\{C_6H_6\}Mo(CO)_3$	120–125	34, 88, 110
$\{C_6H_5F\}Mo(CO)_3$		88
$\{C_6H_5CH_3\}Mo(CO)_3$	127–128	88
$\{1,4\text{-}(CH_3)_2C_6H_4\}Mo(CO)_3$	139–140	88, 92
$\{1,3,5\text{-}(CH_3)_3C_6H_3\}Mo(CO)_3$	150d	34, 80, 110
$\{1,4\text{-}CH_3C_6H_4CH(CH_3)_2\}Mo(CO)$		68
$\{C_{12}H_8\}Mo(CO)_3$	163–185	9
$\{C_{12}H_8\}Mo_2(CO)_6$		9
$\{C_6H_6\}W(CO)_3$	140–145	34
$\{C_6H_5CH_3\}W(CO)_3$	140–142	89
$\{1,4\text{-}(CH_3)_2C_6H_4\}W(CO)_3$	143–145	89
$\{1,3,5\text{-}(CH_3)_3C_6H_3\}W(CO)_3$	160	34
$\{1,4\text{-}CH_3C_6H_4CH(CH_3)_2\}W(CO)_3$		68
$\{C_6H_6\}Cr[(CH_3)_2SO](CO)_2$	133	96
$\{C_6H_6\}Cr(CO)_2(C_5H_5N)$		96
$\{C_6H_6\}Cr(CO)_2(C_7H_{11}N)$ cyclohexyl isonitrile	90d	98
$\{C_6H_6\}Cr(CO)_2(C_9H_7N)$ quinoline	90d	98
$\{C_6H_6\}Cr(CO)_2[P(C_6H_5)_3]$	233	96
$\{1,3,5\text{-}(CH_3)_3C_6H_3\}Cr(C_2H_4)(CO)_2$	100d	32
$\{1,3,5\text{-}(CH_3)_3C_6H_3\}Cr(CO)_2[(CH_3)_2SO]$	150	96
$\{1,3,5\text{-}(CH_3)_3C_6H_3\}Cr(CO)_2(C_5H_5N)$	100d	96
$\{1,3,5\text{-}(CH_3)_3C_6H_3\}Cr(CO)_2(C_9H_7N)$ quinoline	70d	98
$\{1,3,5\text{-}(CH_3)_3C_6H_3\}Cr(CO)_2[(C_6H_5)_3P]$	222	96
$\{1,4\text{-}(CH_3OOC)_2C_6H_4\}Cr(CO)_2(CH_3CN)$		95
$\{1,4\text{-}(CH_3OOC)_2C_6H_4\}Cr(CO)_2(C_5H_5N)$	147	96
$\{1,4\text{-}(CH_3OOC)_2C_6H_4\}Cr(CO)_2(C_5H_{11}N)$	140d	96
$\{1,4\text{-}(CH_3OOC)_2C_6H_4\}Cr(CO)_2(C_6H_5NH_2)$	90d	95
$\{1,4\text{-}(CH_3OOC)_2C_6H_4\}Cr(CO)_2(C_6H_5CN)$	121	95
$\{1,4\text{-}(CH_3OOC)_2C_6H_4\}Cr(CO)_2(C_7H_{11}N)$ cyclohexylisonitrile	126	98
$\{1,4\text{-}(CH_3OOC)_2C_6H_4\}Cr(CO)_2(C_9H_7N)$ quinoline	166	95
$\{1,4\text{-}(CH_3OOC)_2C_6H_4\}Cr(CO)_2[(C_6H_5)_3P]$	160	96
$\{(CH_3)_6C_6\}Cr(CO)_2[(CH_3)_2SO]$	167	98
$\{(CH_3)_6C_6\}Cr(CO)_2(C_9H_7N)$ quinoline		98
$\{(CH_3)_6C_6\}Cr(CO)_2[(C_6H_5)_3P]$	257	98
$\{1,3,5\text{-}(CH_3)_3C_6H_3\}Mo(C_2H_4)(CO)_2$	85d	32

REFERENCES

1. BOSTON, J. L., D. W. A. SHARP, and G. WILKINSON, *J. Chem. Soc.*, **1962**, 3488.
2. BROWN, D. A., and H. SLOAN, *J. Chem. Soc.*, **1962**, 3849.
3. BROWN D. A., J. P. HARGADEN, C. M. McMULLIN, N. GOGAN, and H. SLOAN, *J. Chem. Soc.*, **1963**, 4914.

4. BUELL, G. R., W. E. MCEWEN, and J. KLEINBERG, *J. Am. Chem. Soc.*, **84**, 40 (1962).
5. CAIS, M., and M. FELDKIMEL, *Tetrahedron Letters*, **13**, 444 (1961).
6. CAIS, M., A. MODIANO, N. TIROSH, and A. EISENSTADT, *Proc. Eighth Intern. Conf. Coord. Chem.*, 1964, 11B3, p. 229.
7. CALDERAZZO, F., *Inorg. Chem.*, **3**, 1207 (1964).
8. CALDERAZZO, F., R. ERCOLI, and A. MANGINI, *Ric. Sci. Riv.*, **29**, 2615 (1959).
9. CHATT, J., R. G. GUY, and H. R. WATSON *J. Chem. Soc.*, **1961**, 2332.
10. CHINI, P., and R. ERCOLI, *Gazz. Chim. Ital.*, **88**, 1170 (1958).
11. CHURCHILL, M. R., and R. MASON, *Proc. Chem. Soc.*, **1963**, 112.
12. COFFIELD, T. H., V. SANDEL, and R. D. CLOSSON, *J. Am. Chem. Soc.*, **79**, 5826 (1957); *Abstracts*, 134th Meeting Am. Chem. Soc., 1958, 58-P.
13. CORRADINI, P., and G. ALLEGRA, *J. Am. Chem. Soc.*, **81**, 2271 (1959); *ibid.*, **82**, 2075 (1960).
14. COTTON, F. A., "Infrared Spectra of Transition Metal Complexes," Chapter 5 of J. LEWIS and R. G. WILKINS, *Modern Coordination Chemistry*, Interscience Publishers, Inc., New York, 1960.
15. COTTON, F. A., W. A. DOLLASE, and J. S. WOOD, *J. Am. Chem. Soc.*, **85**, 1543 (1963).
16. CRAM, D. J., and D. I. WILKINSON, *J. Am. Chem. Soc.*, **82**, 5721 (1960).
17. DAUBEN, H. J., and D. J. BERTELLI, *J. Am. Chem. Soc.*, **83**, 497 (1961).
18. DAUBEN, H. J., and L. R. HONNEN, *J. Am. Chem. Soc.*, **80**, 5570 (1958).
19. DAVISON, A., W. MCFARLANE, L. PRATT, and G. WILKINSON, *J. Chem. Soc.*, **1962**, 3653.
20. DEHM, H. C., and J. C. W. CHIEN, *J. Am. Chem. Soc.*, **82**, 4429 (1960).
21. DEVRIES, H., *Rec. Trav. Chim.*, **81**, 359 (1962).
22. ENGEBRETSON, G., and R. E. RUNDLE, *J. Am. Chem. Soc.*, **85**, 481 (1963).
23. ERCOLI, R., F. CALDERAZZO, and A. ALBEROLA, *Chim. Ind.* (Milan), **41**, 975 (1959).
24. ERCOLI, R., F. CALDERAZZO, and E. MANTICA, *Chim. Ind.* (Milan), **41**, 404 (1959).
25. ERCOLI, R., and A. MANGINI, *Ric. Sci. Riv.*, **28**, 2135 (1958).
26. FISCHER, E. O., and O. BECKERT, *Angew Chem.*, **70**, 744 (1958).
27. FISCHER, E. O., and R. BÖTTCHER, *Chem. Ber.*, **89**, 2397 (1956).
28. FISCHER, E. O., and R. D. FISCHER, *Angew. Chem.*, **72**, 919 (1960).
29. FISCHER, E. O., G. JOOS, and W. MEER, *Z. Naturforsch.*, **13b**, 456 (1958).
30. FISCHER, E. O., and N. KRIEBITZSCH, *Z, Naturforsch.*, **15b**, 465 (1960).
31. FISCHER, E. O., N. KRIEBITZSCH, and R. D. FISCHER, *Chem. Ber.*, **92**, 3214 (1959).
32. FISCHER, E. O., and P. KUZEL, *Z. Naturforsch.*, **16b**, 475 (1961).
33. FISCHER, E. O., and K. ÖFELE, *Chem. Ber.*, **90**, 2532 (1957).
34. FISCHER, E. O., and K. ÖFELE, *Z. Naturforsch.*, **13b**, 458 (1958).
35. FISCHER, E. O., and K. ÖFELE, *Chem. Ber.*, **91**, 2395 (1958).
36. FISCHER, E. O., K. ÖFELE, H. ESSLER, W. FRÖHLICH, P. MORTENSEN, and W. SEMMLINGER, *Chem. Ber.*, **91**, 2763 (1958); *Z. Naturforsch.*, **13b**, 458 (1958).
37. FISCHER, E. O., and U. PIESBERGER, *Z. Naturforsch.*, **11b**, 758 (1956).
38. FISCHER, E. O., and S. SCHREINER, *Chem. Ber.*, **92**, 938 (1959).
39. FISCHER, E. O., and W. SEMMLINGER, *Naturwissenschaften*, **48**, 525 (1961).
40. FISCHER, R. D., *Chem. Ber.*, **93**, 165 (1960).
41. FISCHER, R. D., *Spectrochim. Acta*, **19**, 842 (1963).
42. FRITZ, H. P., in F. G. A. STONE and R. WEST (eds.), *Advances in Organometallic Chemistry*, vol. 1, Academic Press, New York, 1964, p. 239.

43. FRITZ, H. P., and J. MANCHOT, Spectrochim. Acta, 18, 171 (1962).
44. FRITZ, H. P., and J. MANCHOT, Z. Naturforsch., 17b, 711 (1962).
45. FRITZ, H. P., and E. F. PAULUS, Z. Naturforsch., 18b, 435 (1963).
46. HARPER, R. J., U.S. Patent 3,073,855, C.A., 60, 562b (1964).
47. HEIN, F., and H. REINERT, Chem. Ber., 93, 2089 (1960).
48. HERBERICH, G. E., and E. O. FISCHER, Chem. Ber., 95, 2803 (1962).
49. HILL, E. A., and J. H. RICHARDS, J. Am. Chem. Soc., 83, 3840 (1961); ibid., 4216 (1961).
50. HÜBEL, W., E. H. BRAYE, A. CLAUSS, E. WEISS, U. KRÜERKE, D. A. BROWN, G. S. D. KING, and C. HOOGZAND, J. Inorg. Nucl. Chem., 9, 204 (1959).
51. HÜBEL, W., and C. HOOGZAND, Chem. Ber., 93, 103 (1960).
52. HUGGINS, D. K., and H. D. KAESZ, Solid State Chemistry, vol. 1, Pergamon Press, Inc. New York, 1964, p. 417.
53. HUMPHREY, R. E., Spectrochim. Acta, 17, 93 (1961).
54. IBERS, J. A., J. Chem. Phys., 40, 3129 (1964).
55. JACKSON, W. R., B. NICHOLLS, and M. C. WHITING, J. Chem. Soc., 1960, 469.
56. JONES, D., L. PRATT, and G. WILKINSON, J. Chem. Soc., 1962, 4458.
57. JONES, D., and G. WILKINSON, J. Chem. Soc., 1964, 2479.
58. KING, R. B., and F. G. A. STONE, J. Am. Chem. Soc., 81, 5263 (1959).
59. KING, R. B., and F. G. A. STONE, Chem. Ind. (London), 1960, 232.
60. KING R. B., and F. G. A. STONE, J. Am. Chem. Soc., 82, 4557 (1960).
61. KREITER, C. G., and H. P. FRITZ, Proc. Eighth Intern. Conf. Coord. Chem., 1964, 6A2, p. 60.
62. KRÜERKE, U., C. HOOGZAND, and W. HÜBEL, Chem. Ber., 94, 2817, 2829 (1961).
63. LIPTAY, W., W. STROHMEIER, and H. HELLMANN, Ber. Bunsenges. Physik. Chem., 68, 91 (1964).
64. LUNDQUIST, R. T., and M. CAIS, J. Org. Chem., 27, 1167 (1962).
65. MANDELBAUM, A., Z. NEUWITH, and M. CAIS, Inorg. Chem., 2, 902 (1963).
66. MANUEL, T. A., Inorg. Chem., 3, 1794 (1964).
67. MANUEL, T. A., S. L. STAFFORD, and F. G. A. STONE, J. Am. Chem. Soc., 83, 3597 (1961).
68. MANUEL, T. A., and F. G. A. STONE, Chem. Ind. (London), 1960, 231.
69. MARKBY, R., H. W. STERNBERG, and J. WENDER, Chem. Ind. (London), 1959, 1381.
70. MARTIN, H., and F. VOHWINKEL, Chem. Ber., 94, 2416 (1961).
71. MATTHEWS, C. N., T. A. MAGEE, and J. H. WOTIZ, J. Am. Chem. Soc., 81, 2273 (1959).
72. MILLS, O. S., and G. ROBINSON, Proc. Chem. Soc., 1964, 187.
73. MUNRO, J. D., and P. L. PAUSON, Proc. Chem. Soc., 1959, 267.
74. MUNRO, J. D., and P. L. PAUSON, J. Chem. Soc., 1961, 3475, 3479.
75. NAKAMURA, A., and M. TSUTSUI, J. Med. Pharm. Chem., 7, 335 (1964), ibid., 6, 795 (1963); Z. Naturforsch., 18b, 666 (1963).
76. NATTA, G., F. CALDERAZZO, and E. SANTAMBROGIO, Chim. Ind. (Milan), 40, 1003 (1958).
77. NATTA, G., R. ERCOLI, and F. CALDERAZZO, Chim. Ind. (Milan), 40, 287 (1958).
78. NATTA, G., G. MAZZANTI, and G. PREGAGLIA, Gazz. Chim. Ital., 89, 2065 (1959) Tetrahedron, 8, 86 (1960).
79. NICHOLLS, B., and M. C. WHITING, Proc. Chem. Soc., 1958, 152.
80. NICHOLLS, B., and M. C. WHITING, J. Chem. Soc., 1959, 551.

81. NICHOLLS, B., and M. C. WHITING, *J. Chem. Soc.*, **1959**, 469.
82. OTSUKA, S., and M. KAWAKAMI, *Chem. Eng. News*, Sept. 14, 1964, 44.
83. RANDALL, E. W., and L. E. SUTTON, *Proc. Chem. Soc.*, **1959**, 93.
84. RIEMSCHNEIDER, R., O. BECKER, and K. FRANZ, *Monatsh. Chem.* **90**, 571 (1959).
85. STERNBERG, H. W., R. MARKBY, and I. WENDER, *J. Am. Chem. Soc.*, **80**, 1009 (1958).
86. STOLZ, I. W., H. HAAS, and R. K. SHELINE, *J. Am. Chem. Soc.*, **87**, 716 (1965).
87. STROHMEIER, W., *Chem. Ber.*, **94**, 2490 (1961).
88. STROHMEIER, W., *Chem. Ber.*, **94**, 3337 (1961).
89. STROHMEIER, W., *Z. Naturforsch.*, **17b**, 566 (1962).
90. STROHMEIER, W., *Z. Naturforsch.*, **17b**, 627 (1962).
91. STROHMEIER, W., *Angew. Chem.*, **76**, 873 (1964).
92. STROHMEIER, W., A. E. HAHGOUB, and D. VON HOBE, *Z. Physik. Chem.* (Frankfurt), **35**, 253 (1962).
93. STROHMEIER, W., and P. HARTMANN, *Z. Naturforsch.*, **18b**, 506 (1963).
94. STROHMEIER, W., and H. HELLMANN, *Ber. Bunsenges. Physik. Chem.*, **67**, 190 (1963).
95. STROHMEIER, W., and H. HELLMANN, *Z. Naturforsch.*, **18b**, 769 (1963).
96. STROHMEIER, W., and H. HELLMANN, *Chem. Ber.*, **96**, 2859 (1963).
97. STROHMEIER, W., and H. HELLMANN, *Ber. Bunsenges. Physik. Chem.*, **68**, 481 (1964).
98. STROHMEIER, W., and H. HELLMANN, *Chem. Ber.*, **97**, 1877 (1964).
99. STROHMEIER, W., and D. VON HOBE, *Ber. Bunsenges. Physik. Chem.*, **64**, 945 (1960).
100. STROHMEIER, W., and D. VON HOBE, *Z. Naturforsch.*, **18b**, 770 (1963).
101. STROHMEIER, W., and D. VON HOBE, *Z. Naturforsch.*, **18b**, 981 (1963).
102. STROHMEIER, W., and H. MITTNACHT, *Z. Physik. Chem.* (Frankfurt), **29**, 339 (1961).
103. STROHMEIER, W., and H. MITTNACHT, *Chem. Ber.*, **93**, 2085 (1960).
104. STROHMEIER, W., and R. MÜLLER, *Z. Physik. Chem.* (Frankfurt), **40**, 86 (1964).
105. STROHMEIER, W., and E. H. STARICCO, *Z. Physik. Chem.* (Frankfurt), **38**, 315 (1963).
106. TATE, D. P., J. M. AUGL, W. M. TITCHEY, B. L. ROSS, and J. G. GRASELLI, *J. Am. Chem. Soc.*, **86**, 3261 (1964).
107. TIERS, L. V. D., *Abstracts 137th Meeting Am. Chem. Soc.*, 1960, 4-O.
108. TSUTSUI, M., and A. NAKAMURA, *Proc. Eighth Intern. Conf. Coord. Chem.*, 1964, 11B4, 232.
109. TYLER, J. K., A. P. COX, and J. SHERIDAN, *Nature*, **183**, 1182 (1959).
110. WERNER, R. P. M., and T. H. COFFIELD, in S. KIRSCHNER (ed.), *Advances in the Chemistry of the Coordination Compounds*, Macmillan Co., New York, 1961, p. 535.
111. WILLEFORD, B. R., and E. O. FISCHER, *Naturwissenschaften*, **51**, 38 (1964).
112. WINKHAUS, G., *Z. Anorg. Allgem. Chem.*, **319**, 404 (1963).
113. WINKHAUS, G., L. PRATT, and G. WILKINSON, *J. Chem. Soc.*, **1961**, 3807.
114. ZEISS, H. (ed.), *Organometallic Chemistry*, Am. Chem. Soc. Monograph No. 147, Reinhold Publishing Corp., 1960.

Appendix: Nomenclature

For clarity, the recommendations of the International Union of Pure and Applied Chemistry* are adhered to in general. The recommendations of W. C. Ferneliusf have been adopted in many instances, although, for ease of reading, the hyphen is used in separating one ligand or type of ligand from another. Thus the reader should more easily be in a position to create an image of the compound in his mind while reading, rather than losing the thread of thought by concentrating on the mechanism of separating syllables in a long complex name.

The benzenoid compound π-bonded to the metal is mentioned first; if more than one is present, they are mentioned in alphabetical order. The numbers *mono, bis, tris,* etc. are used before the organic ligand.

If other ligands are present, these follow the benzenoid ligand and are separated from this and other types of ligands by hyphens. The order of ligands will be benzenoid, other π-bonded organic ligands and inorganic ligands (positive, neutral, negative with the usual endings). Organic ligands *sigma*-bonded to the metal will appear immediately before the metal without separation. The name of the element will appear last with the designation of oxidation-state numerals appearing in parenthesis. The metal will have its usual ending in cationic and neutral complexes and will end in *-ate* in anionic complexes.

In writing formulas, braces will be used to encompass the benzenoid compounds which are π-bonded to transition metals. Formal oxidation states will appear in roman numerals as superscripts to the metal while arabic numbers will be used to designate charges (+ or −) of complex ions.

* W. P. Jorissen, H. Bassett, A. Damiens, F. Fichter, and H. Remy, *J. Am. Chem. Soc.*, **63**, 889 (1941).

† W. C. Fernelius, in "Chemical Nomenclature," *Advan. Chem. Ser.*, No. 8, p. 9 (American Chemical Society, Washington, 1953).

EXAMPLES

Formula	*Name*
$\{C_6H_6\}_2Cr^0$	bis-benzene-chromium(0)
$\{C_6H_6\}_2Cr^I$	bis-benzene-chromium(I) iodide
$[\{(C_6H_5)_2\}_2Cr^I]^+[Cr^{III}(NH_3)_2(SCN)_4]^-$	bis-biphenyl-chromium(I) diammine-tetrathiocyanato-chromate(II) (also called reineckate)
$\{C_6H_6\}\{(C_6H_5)_2\}Cr^0$	benzene-biphenyl-chromium(0)
$\{C_6H_6\}Cr(CO)_3$	benzene-tricarbonyl-chromium(0)
$[\{C_6H_6\}(C_5H_5)W^{II}]^+PF_6^-$	benzene-cyclopentadienyl-tungsten(II) hexafluorophosphate
$[\{1,3,5\text{-}(CH_3)_3C_6H_3\}_2V]^+I^-$	bis-(1,3,5-trimethylbenzene)-vanadium(I) iodide or bis-mesitylene-vanadium(I) iodide
$[\{C_6H_6\}V^I(CO)_4]^+PF_6^-$	benzene-tetracarbonyl-vanadium(I) hexafluorophosphate
$[\{1,4\text{-}(CH_3)_2C_6H_4\}V(CO)_4]^+[V(CO)_6]^-$	p-xylene-tetracarbonyl-vanadium(I) hexacarbonylvanadate(−I)
$[C_6H_5CH_2Cr(H_2O)_5]^{2+}(ClO_4)_2^{2-}$	penta-aquabenzylchromium(III) perchlorate
$Na_3^{3+}[(C_6H_5CH_2)Co(CN)_5]^{3-}$	sodium pentacyano-benzylcobaltate(III)

Author Index

Numbers in roman type refer to pages. Numbers in italic type (in parenthesis) are keys to the end-of-chapter References following those pages.

Subject Index